I0796595

AMAZING CHURCHES

AMAZING CHURCHES

MICHAEL KERRIGAN

This new edition first published in 2026

First edition published in 2020

Published by
Amber Books Ltd
United House
North Road
London N7 9DP
United Kingdom
www.amberbooks.co.uk
Facebook: amberbooks
YouTube: amberbooksltd
Instagram: amberbooksltd
X(Twitter): @amberbooks

ISBN: 978-1-83886-690-7

Project Editor: Kieron Connolly
Designer: Gary Webb and Mark Batley
Picture Research: Terry Forshaw

Printed in China

Contents

Introduction

A powerful ruler's monument, an assertion of communal identity, a colonialist vaunt… a church is never really just a church. Some Christians feel that it ought to be, that they should be able to gather in each other's homes or hired rooms – just as the Disciples did at Pentecost. To them, domes and spires, aisles and arched windows are so much frippery. They have a case, though where

Christian leaders have preferred to take a more worldly role in a wider society, the need for a more imposing public face was felt.

Scripturally justified or not, their decision has given the world some of its most beautiful buildings, its most splendid interiors, its most atmospheric spaces – an inspiration not just to Christians but to humankind. And whatever vanities they may represent, churches can't help but be uplifting. Ungodly as many of us may be, we still find it reassuring to know that some accommodation is being made to the idea of something more – to a wisdom and a truth that transcend our own.

ABOVE:
Iglesia de la Merced, Ushuaia, Tierra del Fuego, Argentina
Ushuaia started life as a penal colony and the convicts who built this church will surely have drawn comfort from its dedication to Our Lady of Mercy, forgiver of sinners and protector of the poor.

OPPOSITE:
North Portal, Chartres Cathedral, Eure-et-Loir, France
This is not just 'decoration' but a sculptuary scripture. Here we see St Anne attended on either side by patriarchs and prophets; above her head, her daughter Mary is received into heavenly glory.

Europe

It may have been born in the Middle East, and in recent times expanded all around the globe, but Christianity grew and came of age in Europe. It hasn't been all love and peace: in the eleventh century, bickering brought the East–West Schism, dividing the Orthodox and Catholic churches, whilst the Reformation of the sixteenth century sowed serious hatreds within the West.

'I never weary of great churches,' wrote the Scottish writer Robert Louis Stevenson. 'Mankind was never so happily inspired as when it made a cathedral.' Heirs to the rancours of the Reformation, Stevenson's strict Presbyterian parents would have been suspicious of the whole idea of a cathedral. To suggest that one church might be more important, more holy than another, implied a lack of devotional democracy.

What their son saw, however, with the fading of his early faith, was that the great historic churches were, on the contrary, collective efforts; the ultimate expressions of shared values and a common creativity. 'I bring not peace but a sword,' Christ said (Matthew 10, 34). And it's true: over millennia many thousands have been slaughtered. But that despite these dissensions we've been capable of coming together to build beautiful churches is a matter for celebration, regardless of our faith – or our scepticism.

OPPOSITE:
Temple of Valadier, Genga, Marche, Italy
Tucked in beneath the raking roof of a limestone cave in the Apennines, this octagonal chapel was constructed as a 'Refuge of Sinners'. Built in 1828, it was commissioned by Pope (and local boy) Leo XII (1760–1829) and designed by the celebrated neo-classical architect Giuseppe Valadier (1762–1839).

PREVIOUS PAGE:

Canterbury Cathedral, Kent, England

St Thomas à Becket (c.1120–70) would have walked these cloisters before his martyrdom; the pilgrims in Chaucer's fourteenth-century *Canterbury Tales* are coming here to see his shrine. Today this beautiful cathedral is most famous as the Mother Church of the worldwide Anglican Communion, a body more than 80 million members strong.

OPPOSITE:

Church of St Mary and All Saints, Chesterfield, Derbyshire, England

An unmistakable landmark, the crooked spire is believed to have been caused by the action of the summer sun on the warmer, southern side, which warped the roof's lead covering and pulled it out of true. There's believed to have been a church here since the end of the ninth century.

TOP LEFT:

Coventry Cathedral, West Midlands, England

Ruined remnants of the old (fifteenth-century) cathedral are still to be seen beside this stunning new one, built in the aftermath of World War II. Taken together, the two churches comprise a moving memorial to the bombing raid of November 1940, which devastated Coventry, and an inspiring symbol of hope, for faith and peace.

LEFT:

Liverpool Metropolitan Cathedral, Merseyside, England

Perceptions are everything. Nominally crown-shaped for its dedication to 'Christ the King', this Catholic cathedral was conceived as an architectural adventure for the space age: futuristic, vaguely rocket-like in form. By the time it was completed in 1967, the Beatles had re-shaped the world's appreciation of their home city and the Metropolitan Cathedral was being praised as a piece of fun and quirky 'pop art'.

ABOVE AND LEFT:

St Materiana's Church, Tintagel, Cornwall, England

Visible for miles up and down this rugged coast, St Materiana's was an invaluable mark for mariners in ages past. It stands on an exposed headland some way outside the village of Tintagel. Believed to have been a fifth-century British princess, Materiana is one of scores of Cornish saints of whom little is known beyond their associations with churches or their commemoration in place-names. Mysteries swirl around this whole area. Tintagel Castle has strong associations with Arthurian legend and early-medieval remains have indeed been found here.

St Materiana's was already old when the Norman font (left) was carved, though the exterior was to be restored and modified over the centuries that followed.

ABOVE AND LEFT:

Rug Chapel, Corwen, Wales

A colourful if contradictory character, William Salesbury (1580–1660) is said to have served as a privateer in the East Indies before becoming the member of parliament for Merioneth in the 1620s. He went on to fight for the Royalist side in the English Civil War (1642–51), mounting a heroic (if ultimately unsuccessful) defence of Denbigh Castle. He built this chapel towards the end of his life. Its dour exterior does nothing to prepare us for the extraordinary wealth of woodcarving and decorative tile-work inside. This was by design, of course, when every one of Salesbury's conservative, ultra-high-church views was a provocation to the new puritanical regime.

ABOVE:
St Anne's Cathedral, Belfast, Northern Ireland
Consecrated in 1904, Belfast's Church of Ireland cathedral is built in the Romanesque style of the early medieval churches, with massive pillars holding up the structure upon rounded arches. Stone-carvings celebrate Northern Ireland's important industries, from shipbuilding and linen production to agriculture.

OPPOSITE:
Sanctuary of Our Lady of Knock, County Mayo, Ireland
In 1879, a group of children and older villagers saw an apparition of Our Lady, attended by St Joseph and St John the Evangelist, outside the old church of the remote little Irish village of Knock. This modern basilica was dedicated in 1976.

LEFT:

Glasgow Cathedral, Scotland

The Reformation reached Scotland slightly late, but when it did it swept through the country with a vengeance. Very few medieval churches were to survive. One of those that did is Glasgow Cathedral.

St Mungo, Glasgow's patron saint, is said to have built a church here in the sixth century. The present gothic building – with its beautifully vaulted aisles, breath-taking arches and stunning stained glass – went up in instalments from the late-twelfth century onwards. God's reproach to modern stereotyping of the city as a noisy, smoky, soulless, industrial centre, this wonderful church reminds us of how long, and humane, its history has been.

NEXT PAGES, ALL PHOTOGRAPHS:

Norwich Cathedral, Norfolk, England

Construction of this cathedral took place between the end of the eleventh century and the middle of the twelfth, though it had to be substantially rebuilt in the thirteenth century after rioting in the city.

The spectacular vaulted ceiling was largely completed in the fifteenth century, as were the sumptuously (and often humorously!) carved wooden choir stalls.

The shapely stone spire was built in 1480. Revenues flooded in throughout this period from pilgrims drawn to the shrine of St William of Norwich (1132–44), a young boy supposedly snatched off the street and sacrificed by the city's Jews.

OPPOSITE:
Westminster Abbey, London, England
Writer G.K. Chesterton (1874–1936) dismissed Westminster Abbey as a 'lumber room', given the amount of inferior statuary cluttering up what had become the nation's shrine to its own history. But this exterior of the north door reminds us how stunning the abbey is. Flying buttresses shifted some of the weight from the walls, allowing space to be spared for stained-glass windows.

ABOVE:
St Paul's Cathedral, London, England
Old St Paul's was an impressive-looking gothic pile built between the eleventh and the fourteenth centuries, but badly neglected when Sir Christopher Wren (1632–1723) began restoration work in the early 1660s. Before renovations commenced, though, the cathedral was substantially destroyed in the Great Fire of London (1666).

As absurd as it would be to say that the medieval cathedral's loss had been a blessing, there's no doubt that, in having to start again from scratch, Wren's baroque masterpiece – the St Paul's we know today – has been a glorious addition to the nation's heritage. With a diameter of 34m (112ft) and a height of 111m (365ft), its great dome was to transform the city's skyline.

TOP LEFT:
Rheims Cathedral, Marne, France
The use of pointed arches and of flying buttresses in church-construction allowed for bigger windows and for interiors flooded with light. And with this came instruction, too, because – like carvings and wall paintings – stained glass can be used to offer a visual scripture for the illiterate.

BOTTOM LEFT:
Chartres Cathedral, Eure-et-Loir, France
Europe's gothic cathedrals could take generations – even centuries – to build. They were triumphs of collective effort, individual workers toiling selflessly away to build something so much greater than the sum of its aesthetic parts.

Chartres is rightly celebrated for the sumptuous stained glass and stone- and wood-carving that have made it one of Europe's foremost medieval churches. But work went on into modern times – and, crucially, the gothic cathedral was sufficiently 'open' in its conception to absorb it. This eighteenth-century altar by Charles-Antoine Bridan (1730–1805), with its baroque representation of the Assumption of the Virgin swept up to heaven by a flight of angels, works unexpectedly well in what is otherwise a gothic space.

OPPOSITE:
Sacré-Cœur Basilica, Paris, France
Standing atop the hill at Montmartre, this great Byzantine-styled basilica was built by France's Catholics as an act of 'national penance'. First for the country's defeat in the Franco–Prussian War (1870–71). And, more controversially, for the ungodly socialism of the workers' uprising which gripped this part of Paris during the 'Commune' of 1871.

LEFT:

Notre-Dame, Paris, France

Today Notre-Dame is a stunning gothic church, but at the start of the modern era it was decaying as inexorably as London's Old St Paul's. In the absence of a fire – and, eventually, of course, in the presence from 1789 of a revolutionary government – the decline continued for a great deal longer than in London.

In the end it took Victor Hugo's novel *Notre-Dame de Paris* (1831), and its charismatic character Quasimodo – the 'Hunchback of Notre-Dame' – to revive interest in the cathedral and restore its fortunes.

The fire of 2019 was a devastating shock to France, but Notre-Dame has come back from the brink before and surely will again.

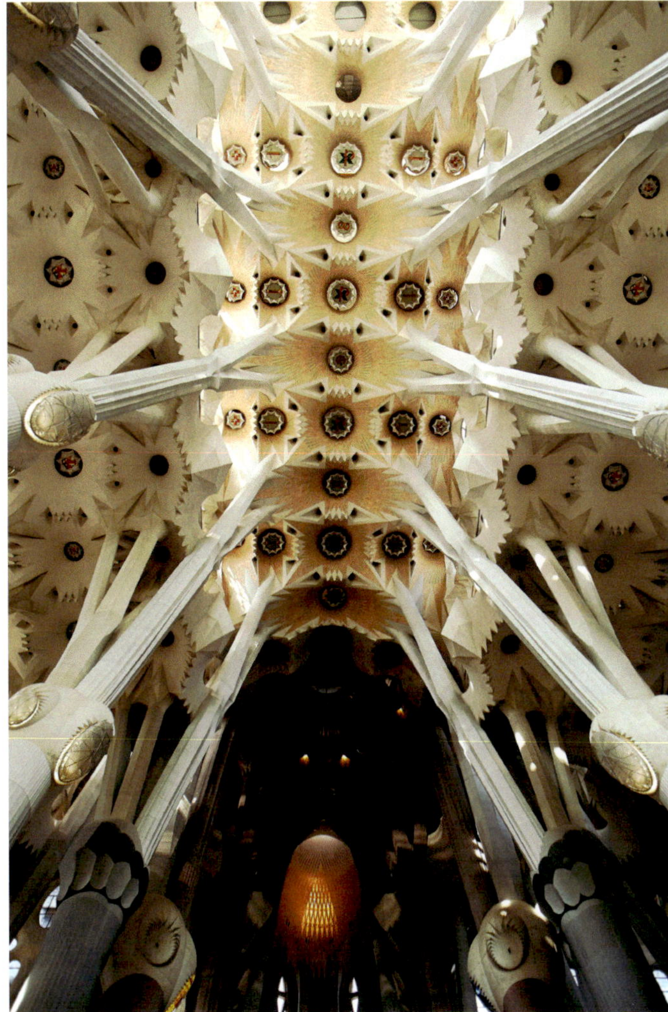

OPPOSITE:
Church of St Roch, Lisbon, Portugal
This understated façade is deliberately deceptive. Inside lies a spectacular interior, all bright baroque-ness, with walls lavishly frescoed between rich marble columns, and saints and angels floating off into *trompe l'oeil* ceilings.

The attempt to startle was intentional, of course. Portugal's first Jesuit Church was at the forefront of the Catholic 'Counter-Reformation' movement. The Catholic Church had been hard hit by the rise of Protestantism, and the more personalized and feeling faith that it fostered. Protestant reformers such as Martin Luther had identified a major unmet need. Art like this was intended to encourage more emotional forms of Catholic devotion, allowing believers to find fulfilment within the Church.

TOP LEFT, BOTTOM LEFT AND ABOVE:
Sagrada Família, Barcelona, Catalonia, Spain
Someone made a cathedral from ice cream and now it's melting! Gothic goes absolutely insane in this, the most instantly recognizable work by Barcelona's most famous architect, Antoni Gaudí (1852–1926). Begun in 1882, it remains unfinished to this day.

For Catalan writer Luis Goytisolo, Sagrada Família – 'the Basilica of the Holy Family' – is profoundly ambiguous. On the one hand, it's gloriously gothic, with so many stunning details that you can hardly apprehend the whole, making it 'an inconclusive temple of unaccustomed perspectives'. On the other, it's the ultimate monument to nineteenth-century conventionality. What could be more bourgeois than a celebration of the family?

Valencia Cathedral, Spain
Originally a gothic construction consecrated in 1238, this great church was given a neoclassical makeover in the 1770s – hence the removal of pinnacles, the structure's general smoothing-over with stucco, and, of course, that stubby-looking sawn-off spire. Look up from inside the cathedral, though, and you see a stunning, star-shaped dome; much of the interior still has a gothic feel, along with elements of neoclassicism and baroque. A slightly chaotic hybrid it may be, but this cathedral 'works' as an inspiring whole.

ABOVE AND OPPOSITE:

Santiago de Compostela Cathedral, Galicia, Spain

St James (Santiago in Spanish), the Apostle of Christ, supposedly came to Spain and preached the Gospel; he returned to the Holy Land but was then martyred. Legend has it that his body was brought back to Galicia in a ship of stone and he was buried at Santiago de Compostela. His grave, forgotten for a time, was rediscovered in the ninth century and a great cathedral raised above his tomb. Another story says that he appeared as a white knight to lead the Spanish army against the Muslim Moors to re-establish Christianity in Spain. This cathedral, an eclectic mix of Romanesque, gothic and baroque, has been an important place of pilgrimage for centuries. The sign above shows pilgrims the Way of the Cross (Via Crucis), whilst (opposite) a statue of St James himself has pride of place on the cathedral's east façade.

OVERLEAF:

Pantheon, Rome, Italy

This was once a pagan temple (the Greek word *Pantheon* means 'all the gods'). Since the seventh century, though, it's been a church – despite its heathen origins – and among the most impressive in the world. Its gigantic, unsupported concrete dome is a miracle of engineering: Brunelleschi was to use it as his model for the one he built in Florence.

LEFT:
Florence Cathedral, Tuscany, Italy
Florence Cathedral, with its gravity-defying dome designed by Filippo Brunelleschi (1377–1446), is often seen as marking the start of the Renaissance in architecture. Its multi-coloured marble panels pick up the terracotta brickwork above and add a whimsical, even confected, note.

TOP AND ABOVE:
St Peter's Basilica, Rome, Italy
The ultimate in churches, the ultimate emblem of the Catholic faith – for better but also for worse, it has been suggested. Indeed, in his eagerness to raise a suitably magnificent monument on the site where the martyred St Peter's bones had, tradition says, been laid, Pope Alexander VII had thrown ethical caution to the wind. In licensing the issue of 'indulgences' – pardons for sins – for money, Martin Luther insisted that Alexander had sold his soul. Either way, the project, completed in 1626, brought together a star-studded cast of Italian Renaissance architects, including Donato Bramante, Michelangelo and – a generation later – Gian Lorenzo Bernini. His astonishing *baldacchino* (above) canopies the papal altar and St Peter's bones.

OPPOSITE:
Agios Nikolaos Church, Protaras, Cyprus
Agios Nikolaos Church (St Nicholas's) is almost literally dazzling in its whiteness, set off as it is by the sky blue of its dome and door – as well as, of course, the blue of the sky itself and the azure Mediterranean in the background. Whitewashing was introduced as a way of reflecting heat away: here an otherwise ordinary little church is transfigured into something miraculously beautiful.

BELOW:
Nea Artaki Church, Euboea, Greece
A little church like this one doesn't just provide a function as a place of worship: it's the emblem of a community's identity and faith.

The Greek Orthodox Church separated off from the Western, Roman Church in 1054, though it had been going its own way for some time before that. Unlike the Catholic Church, the Greek Orthodox Church, along with other Eastern Orthodox Churches, has no supreme pontiff, but a Holy Synod of senior bishops.

RIGHT:

St Stephen's Cathedral, Vienna, Austria

Wild gothic and austere Romanesque meet in a cathedral full of beautiful, beguiling features, but the undoubted *pièce de résistance* is the roof. Almost a quarter of a million tiles have been used to pick out elaborate lozenged mosaic patterns – and, in places, pictorial designs. The double-headed eagle of the old Austrian Empire may be seen on one side, for example; the city's coat of arms on the other.

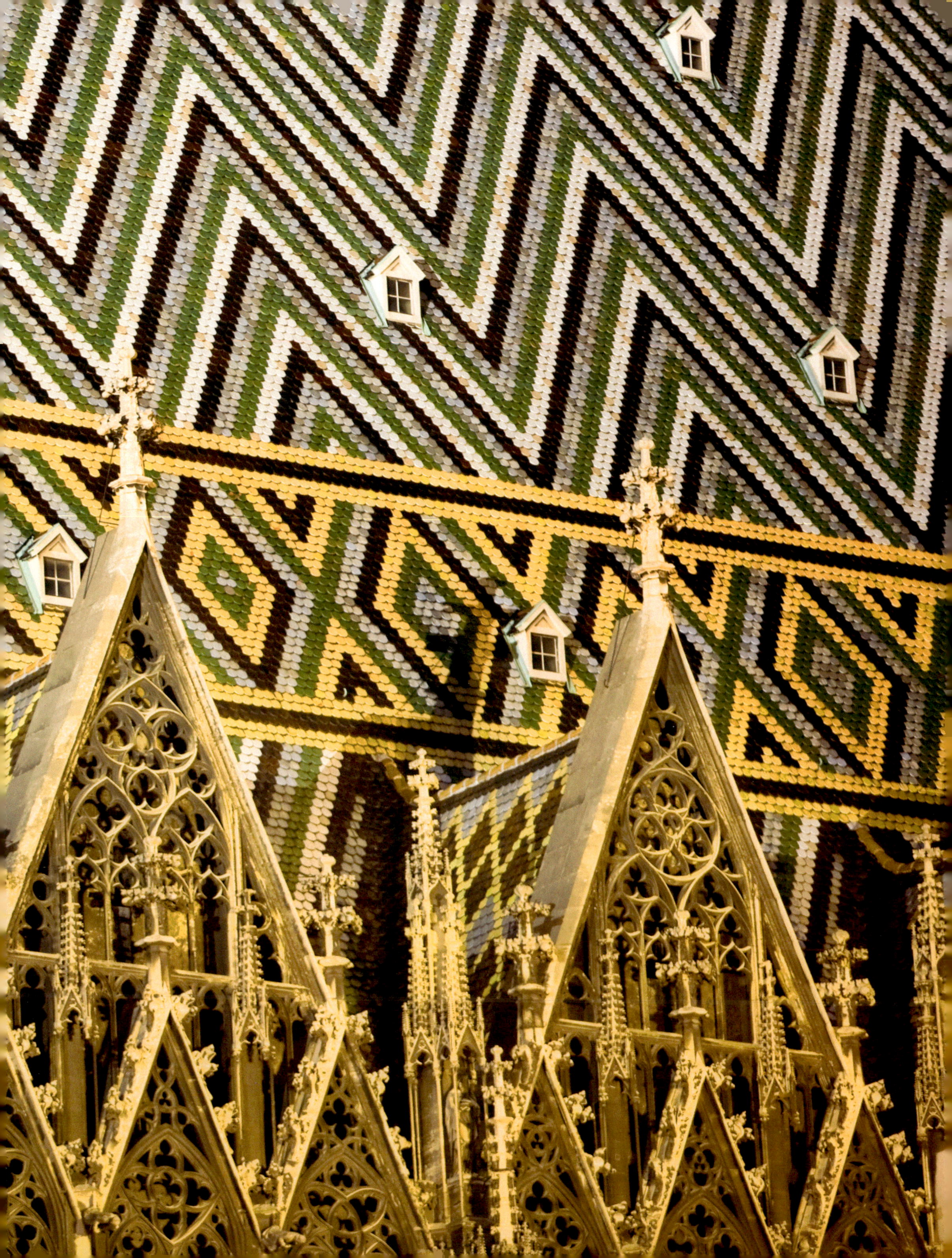

ABOVE AND OPPOSITE:
Frauenkirche, Dresden, Saxony, Germany
The beautiful Lutheran Frauenkirche (Church of Our Lady) was first built in the eighteenth century. Its high dome is awe-inspiring in both its scale and grace. And in its strength, too: it very nearly survived the Allied bombing raid on Dresden in February 1945, but in firestorm temperatures of 1000°C (1832°F) it finally collapsed, and was left a ruin.

After the war, East Germany's Communist rulers didn't recognize any sanctity in the site. Even so, between inefficiency on the one hand and, on the other, a certain awkward deference to the unease of (even non-religious) Dresdeners, they didn't clear away the rubble as they'd once intended. It lay there, indeed, until 1989 when the people of a reunified Germany decided that the Frauenkirche should be restored. The restoration was completed in 2005.

MARTIN LUTHER

LEFT:
Bamberg Cathedral, Bavaria, Germany
The blessed (on the left) offer prayerful thanks; the damned (on the right) are dragged away by demons, or weep in abject anguish as they face the fires of Hell. This sculpted scene, on the cathedral's 'Princes' Portal', sets out the eschatological realities of thirteenth-century faith. And they were realities to men and women in the Middle Ages – not metaphors, nor allegories. Death, Judgement, Heaven and Hell; this was where it was all going to lead. This was what religion, and the religious life, were all about.

NEXT PAGE, LEFT:
Cologne Cathedral, North Rhine-Westphalia, Germany
The sense of peace is extraordinary – truly extraordinary, given that an estimated 20,000 visitors a day come to Cologne to see one of Europe's most breathtakingly beautiful gothic churches. Although building began in the thirteenth century, momentum was lost and it was left unfinished until the medieval plans were used to complete it in the 1880s.

This view highlights the vertiginous vaulting – among the highest in the world. As elsewhere, external flying buttresses help take the strain. A gilded bronze-and-silver reliquary, believed to hold sacred relics of the biblical Three Kings, takes pride of place in the cathedral.

NEXT PAGE, RIGHT:
Hallgrimskirkja, Reykjavik, Iceland
It could almost be a mountain or a rocky crag, its surface stepped by erosion or striated by glacial abrasure as it rises up out of the icy earth, its stone face blue with cold against a golden evening sky.

Standing 74.5m (244ft) tall, Iceland's leading Lutheran church, completed in 1986, towers over the country's capital city.

TOP LEFT:

Borgund Stave Church, Sogn og Fjordane, Norway

Hundreds of 'stave churches' like this were built across Norway in the twelfth and thirteenth centuries. All-wooden in construction, they had timber frames, were walled with interlocking planks (or 'staves') and roofed with wooden shingles. Carved dragon-heads give the gables on this one a 'Viking' look. It's now part of the Lutheran Church of Norway.

BOTTOM LEFT:

Stensele Church, Västerbotten, Sweden

The village of Stensele can claim to have Sweden's biggest wood-built church. The story goes that its builders prepared seating for every single man, woman and child in an extensive parish. Completed in 1885, it can seat 2000 people.

RIGHT:

Temppeliaukio Church, Helsinki, Finland

The main body of this Lutheran church was carved out of the solid rock then built up a little at the sides and roofed over into an amphitheatre-like space. As we see here, it is often used for concerts.

ETC VIRG MARTYRUM

OPPOSITE:

Church of St Peter and St Paul, Vilnius, Lithuania

The Church of St Peter and St Paul looks like it might be made of icing, an architectural wedding-cake. Really, though, it's a symphony in stucco. Its grandeur recalls the days when, in the early years of the eighteenth century, Vilnius belonged to a powerful Polish–Lithuanian Commonwealth. This church is packed with plaster statuary: to the left of the main door we see Death with his scythe, to the right St Christopher carrying the infant Christ. Figures of Apostles and martyrs line the nave.

TOP RIGHT:

St Ignatius Rock Chapel, Všemily, Bohemia, Czech Republic

It isn't clear who built this chapel or why, though it's first mentioned in local records fairly recently, in 1835. The whole thing has been hollowed out of an enormous block of sandstone. Any connection with the Jesuits (the Society of Jesus, which Ignatius Loyola founded) remains obscure. The chapel seems to have been built privately, and since then maintained by pious locals.

BOTTOM RIGHT:

Church of Our Lady before Týn, Prague, Bohemia, Czech Republic

This gothic church in Prague's Old Town was built in the fourteenth and fifteenth centuries. Inside, with some medieval exceptions, the overall look is of baroque. The combination – or counterpoint – of architectural styles actually seems to work quite well.

OPPOSITE:

Greek Catholic Church, Csenger, Hungary

The Greek Catholic Church follows the Eastern Orthodox rite in its services, but looks to the organization and authority of Rome. It's no surprise, then, to see this church, in Hungary's far northeastern corner, reflecting that ambivalence architecturally. Worldwide, the Church is tiny. Even in Csenger County, it includes only 11–12 per cent of the local population.

LEFT:

Ieud Hill Church, Maramures, Romania

This area of northern Romania has almost a hundred traditional wood-built churches: they're made from logs, rather than from planking or from boards. Squat and often very small, this kind of building is marked out by its slim, shapely bell-tower and a roof that strikes the outsider as seeming too big for the church. Inside they tend to be decorated with (often rough and ready) wall paintings.

NEXT PAGE:

Basilica of Our Lady of Lichen, Greater Poland Voivodeship, Poland

One of the world's largest churches, this basilica was built in the 1990s to house a famous icon of Our Lady of Sorrows, Queen of Poland. The painting appeared spontaneously in 1813, it's said, when Tomasz Klossowski, badly wounded in the wars against Napoleon, prayed in desperation to the Virgin Mary. She healed him, helping him home to his family. Many more were subsequently to be cured by her icon.

RIGHT:

Kalyazin Bell Tower, Uglich Reservoir, Kalyazin, Tver Oblast, Russia

For Karl Marx, notoriously, religion had been 'the opium of the people'. Fuddled by its illusory comforts – and beguiled by its promise of relief in an imaginary 'next life' – religion reconciled the poor to their oppression and exploitation. Soviet Communism hoped to sweep away all such benighted superstitions. And how better to do it than with ambitious engineering schemes?

The construction of the Uglich Dam (1936–9) would show what humanity was capable of creating unassisted. And it would generate electricity, to provide real comfort in this life. It was a happy accident that the reservoir it formed would also drown a wide area of valley – including two historic monasteries. The belltower of St Nicholas's, built at the end of the eighteenth century, was left standing high above the waters. For Stalin's comrades this emblematized the supersession of the old beliefs; for the faithful, on the contrary, it represents their endurance.

OPPOSITE:

St Basil's Cathedral, Moscow, Russia

With its gaudy onion spires, outlandishly ornate façades and eye-assaulting interior, St Basil's proclaims Russia's pride in its unique culture and spirituality. It was built to commemorate the conquests of Ivan the Terrible (1547–84), construction beginning in 1555, though it was not completed until 1679.

North America

The first thing life in the New World did for successive generations of European immigration was create a profound nostalgia for the old one. Nowhere was this more strikingly apparent than in the appearance of its churches. This is understandable enough, in light of the fact that, in the US especially, many of the earliest colonists arrived in more or less unwilling flight from religious persecution. (The 'Pilgrim Fathers', who in 1620 arrived in Plymouth, Massachusetts, were only the most famous of these groups.)

But the feeling seems to have been just as strong among the later waves of immigrants who made the westward journey over successive centuries. Again, this is not surprising, given the powerful and intimate psychological hold religious beliefs tend to maintain as aspects of what we'd nowadays characterize as 'identity'.

Collective as well as individual identity: immigrants adrift in a new and alien society found safety in numbers and security in mutual help of a kind which very quickly became associated with the different churches. If the effort to fund and construct a new church gave people a common purpose, the completed building became a badge of status, a sign that a struggling community had established itself, made its mark.

OPPOSITE:
St Patrick's Cathedral, New York City, USA
A church may be a 'house of God', but it's also the habitation of a human spirit, the identity of the community that constructed it. Nowhere is this more obviously so than in the high church of Irish America, built just a decade after the Great Famine (1845–49) drove so many emigrants to US shores.

ABOVE:
**Trinity Church,
New York City, USA**
Although dwarfed by skyscrapers around it, this episcopal church can still stand proud. Since the 1840s, it has emblematized the fact that – even in the heart of New York's Financial District – we can still aspire to something more than money.

RIGHT:
**St Patrick's Cathedral,
New York City, USA**
It's hard to remember that, when first constructed, St Patrick's stood on a patch of waste-ground some way outside New York City. Architect James Renwick modelled his career-pinnacle project on Cologne Cathedral in Germany.

St Joseph's Oratory of Mount Royal, Montreal, Quebec, Canada
A mosaic of multi-coloured candles represents the prayers of faithful pilgrims and pronounces St Joseph the patron of this church, the central shrine of French–Canadian Catholicism. Brother André Bessette began its construction in 1904: his heart is held in a reliquary here. Many claim to have been cured after visits to his church. In 2010, Bessette was canonized by Pope Benedict XVI.

DU TOMBEAU DU FRERE ANDRE

Basilica of St John the Baptist, St John's, Newfoundland and Labrador, Canada
In the 1830s, when the Basilica of St John the Baptist was built, St John's was three-quarters Irish. This basilica was an affirmation of patriotic pride and defiance against the British establishment in Newfoundland – hence the recruitment of both an architect, contractors and craftsmen from Ireland, as well as the importation of Galway limestone and Leinster granite for the basilica's construction.

ABOVE:
First Congregational Church of Litchfield, Connecticut, USA
Congregationalism rejects the hierarchical rule of older churches in the Catholic tradition: each community is essentially self-governing.

LEFT:
Washington National Cathedral, Washington DC, USA
Frederick Hart designed this tympanum above the main door of America's National Cathedral. Called *Ex Nihilo* ('Out of Nothing'), it represents the creation of humankind.

RIGHT:
Trinity Church, Boston, Massachusetts, USA
Architect Henry Hobson Richardson (1838–86) so loved this kind of early medieval pastiche that it became known as 'Richardsonian Romanesque'.

BLESSING AND HONOUR AND GLORY

Trinity Church, Boston, Massachusetts, USA
Do not, said Jesus, be like 'the foolish man who built his house on sand' (Matthew 7, 27), but Henry Hobson Richardson wasn't listening. His architectural skill was greater than his knowledge of the scriptures. This massive, solid-looking monument is lifted up above the semi-liquid reclaimed land of Boston's Back Bay district by 4400 wooden piles.

St Philip's Church, Charleston, South Carolina, USA

For the outsider, at least, St Philip's has a faintly incongruous air, as though one of Christopher Wren's churches had been whisked up from its wet and chilly London home and plonked down in this balmy, southern setting.

Charlestoners take a different view: with its three pedimented porticos and its tapering sectioned spire, this church is essential to the local scene.

It has been a landmark since the middle of the nineteenth century – literally, given that for many years its spire doubled as a lighthouse for shipping off this stretch of the South Carolina coast.

STOP
ALL WAY
ONE WAY

ABOVE:
St Josaphat, Milwaukee, Wisconsin, USA
Rome meets Milwaukee in what amounts to a miniature St Peter's. St Josaphat's expresses the pride of the local Polish population who, by the 1890s, numbered 60,000. Ironically, the size of the city's German population may have had more bearing on the Poles' ambition: they had to try harder to assert themselves. Costs were lessened by bringing 50 trainloads of second-hand masonry from Chicago, where the main post office had just been pulled down.

RIGHT:
Cathedral Basilica of St Louis, Missouri, USA
If you think the exterior's impressive, just wait till you step inside and see the extraordinary sumptuousness of this cathedral. Some 7700 square metres (82,000 square feet) of mosaics extend over just about every surface. Simply to stand here is to have an epiphanic vision. Building sublimity takes time: whilst the vast external shell of this basilica went up in a mere 19 years (1907–26), the interior wasn't completed until 1988.

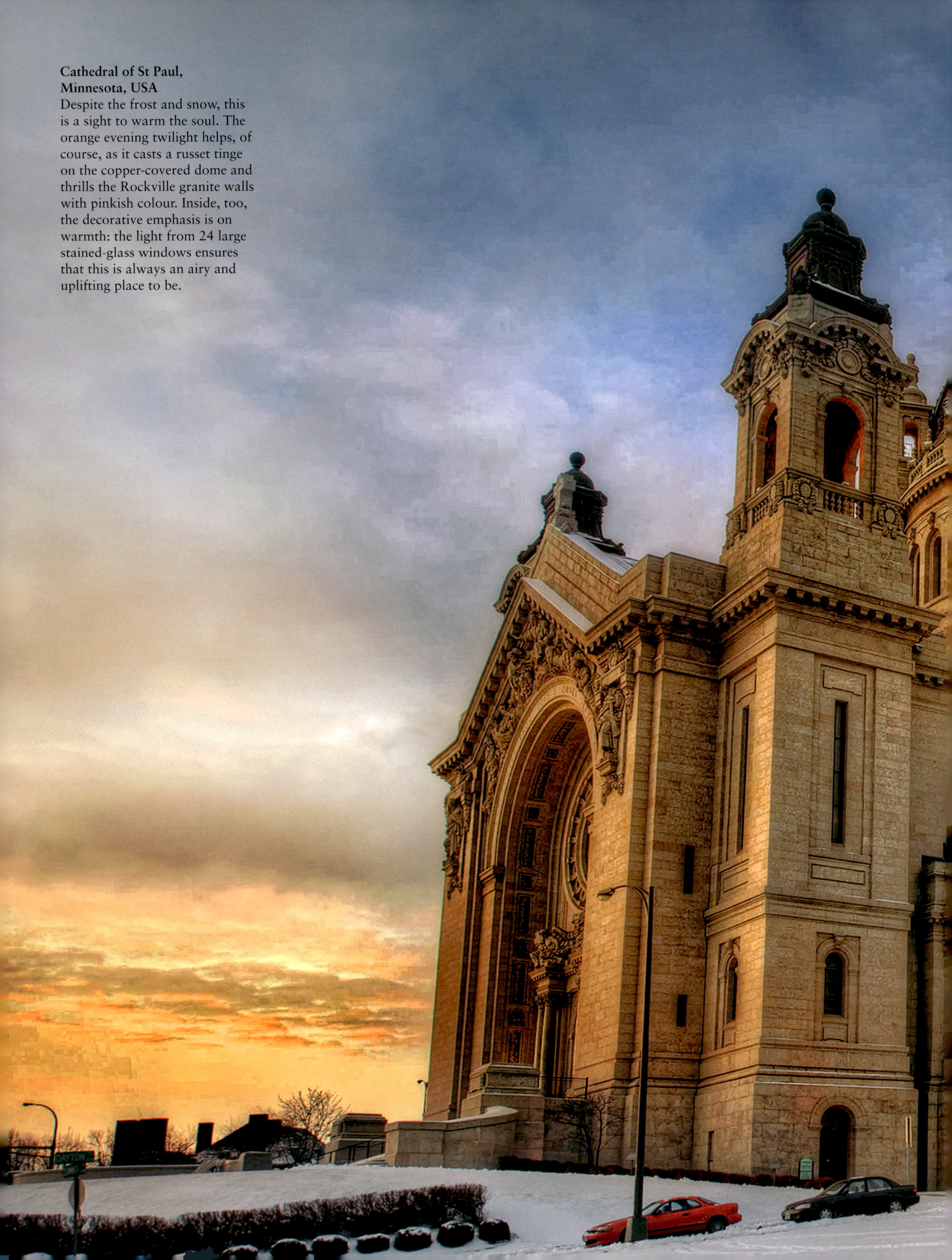

Cathedral of St Paul, Minnesota, USA

Despite the frost and snow, this is a sight to warm the soul. The orange evening twilight helps, of course, as it casts a russet tinge on the copper-covered dome and thrills the Rockville granite walls with pinkish colour. Inside, too, the decorative emphasis is on warmth: the light from 24 large stained-glass windows ensures that this is always an airy and uplifting place to be.

ST. PAUL
FATHER DAMIEN
ST. JOAN OF ARC

LEFT:
Cathedral of St Helena, Montana, USA
The vertical dimension is accented in the design of St Helena's. Its tall, twin spires tower to a height of 70m (230ft), and everything else seems to be stretched up and down as well. Hence this elongated Apostle Paul, lanky beanpole Father Damien (canonized in 1995 for his work among Hawaii's lepers a hundred years before), and this super-slimline Joan of Arc.

ABOVE:
The Church of the Holy Ascension, Unalaska, Aleutian Islands, Alaska, USA
Alaska was a colony of Russia's for well over a century and there has been an Orthodox church on this site for 200 years. The Aleuts took to Christianity with immense enthusiasm. Their faith became essential to their identity. Their evacuation during World War II allowed the church to fall into disrepair and dilapidation. Since then, however, it has been lovingly restored.

OVERLEAF:
St Benedict's Catholic Church, Honaunau, Hawaii, USA
In the early 1900s, Father John Veighe, parish priest of Honaunau, took it upon himself to repaint the inside of his church. Not just a lick of magnolia, though, he created a spectacular neo-gothic phantasmagoria, with *trompe l'oeil* arches, vaulting and beautifully painted frescos, making a soaring, spacious impression of a medieval cathedral out of his boxy, modern, wood-built church.

Kea

Aole

St Benedict's Catholic Church, Honaunau, Hawaii, USA
Father Veighe's wall paintings inside St Benedict's may have been artistic esprit and a spiritual offering, and it's rightly observed that the biblical scenes would have brought instruction to his largely illiterate flock. Surely, though, they stemmed as well from homesickness for his native Belgium? As lush as Honaunau may be, it wasn't home.

STEWARDSHIP

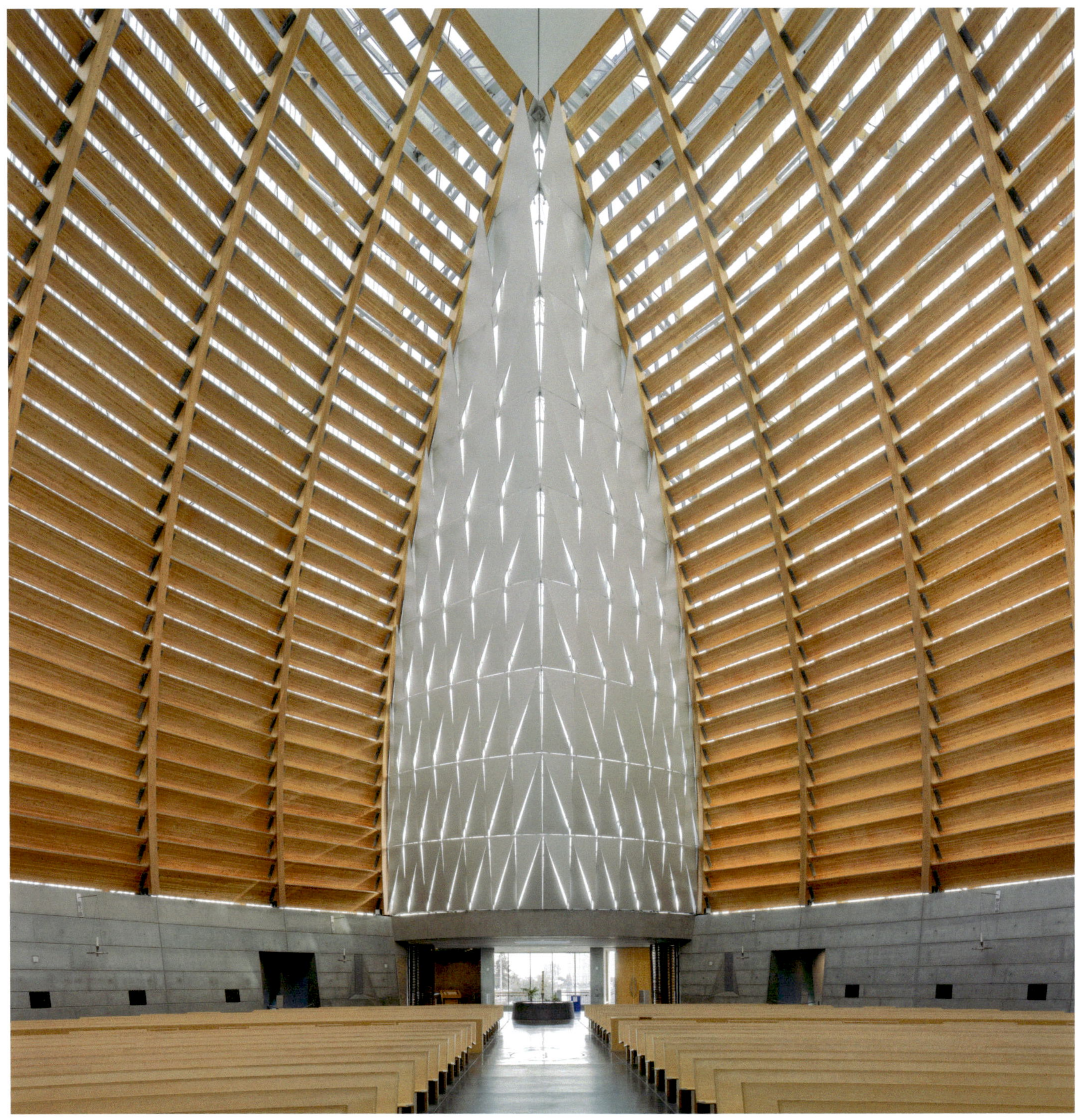

ABOVE:
Cathedral of Christ the Light, Oakland, California, USA
'Glory be to God for dappled things,' wrote the Jesuit priest-poet Gerard Manley Hopkins (1844–89), celebrating 'all things counter, original, spare, strange'. Oakland's cathedral is all these. Architect Craig W. Harman said that he sought the effect of light filtering down 'through a canopy of redwood trees'.

OPPOSITE TOP RIGHT:
Grace Cathedral, San Francisco, California, USA
So artistically rich is Italy's Florence Cathedral that even its medieval baptistery doors are a masterpiece — and copies of them are important artworks. It was during the refurbishment of Florence Cathedral after World War II that the moulds for Grace Cathedral's casts were made. Clockwise from top left, these panels show the stories of Noah, Abraham, Joseph and Isaac.

OPPOSITE BOTTOM RIGHT:
Mission Basilica San Diego de Alcalá, San Diego, California, USA
Not until the 1760s, with the Russians pushing down from Alaska, did the Spanish feel the need to make their presence felt in this part of New Spain. Junipero Serra (1713–84) carried out a series of proselytizing sweeps in California. This was the first mission that he established.

San Diego California Temple, California, USA
'For behold, I have accepted this house...' says the Doctrine & Covenants of the Church of Jesus Christ of the Latter Day Saints. 'And I shall manifest myself to my people in mercy in this house.'

Every church is holy, but the Mormon Temple isn't public in quite the same way that even the most illustrious cathedral is. The Saints have open meeting houses and reach out to the public in other ways, but their temples are reserved for initiates.

LEFT AND ABOVE:
Chapel of the Holy Cross, Sedona, Arizona, USA
A visit to New York in the 1930s inspired Marguerite Brunswig Staude twice over. As a Catholic, she was thrilled by the grandeur of St Patrick's Cathedral. As a sculptor, she revelled in the technological achievement of the Empire State Building. She came away with the hope of a design so sublime that it would almost compel reverence – 'that God may come to life in the souls of all men and be a living reality.'

It's hard to imagine a more stunning church in a more spectacular setting than this chapel, carved into one of the red rock bluffs of Staude's home state. Built between 1955 and 1956, it became a Catholic chapel, but has no services: its builder wanted it to be a place for general, non-denominational prayer and reflection.

OVERLEAF:
Auditorium, Salt Lake Temple, Utah, USA
'And daily in the temple, and in every house, they ceased not to teach and preach Jesus Christ' (Acts 5, 42). But for Mormons (members of the Church of Jesus Christ of the Latter Day Saints), these are two very separate spheres. Only faithful members are admitted to the Temple itself – a sort of Holy of Holies. The Church welcomes others in auditoriums, like the 21,000-seater here.

LEFT:
Lutheran Church, New Sweden, Texas, USA
As its name suggests, this church was founded by immigrants from Sweden. They came in the 1870s, bringing their Lutheran religion with them. Like so many immigrants before them, they grew in confidence as the years went by. Their church to begin with bore the name of Manor, the nearest town. Only in 1887 was it retitled 'New Sweden'.

OPPOSITE, TOP RIGHT:
San Fernando de Bexar Cathedral, San Antonio, Texas, USA
The city of San Antonio grew up out of the tiny town of San Fernando de Béxar – Texas's first official civil settlement, founded in 1731 and named after the future Fernando VI of Spain. Though the present neo-gothic structure was built in the 1860s, it includes walls from the original San Fernando's church.

OPPOSITE, BOTTOM LEFT AND RIGHT:
Thorncrown Chapel, Arkansas, USA
Paris's Sainte-Chapelle (1248) is one of the undisputed treasures of medieval architecture, stunning in its show of painted decoration and stained glass. It isn't big, and from the outside it presents the appearance of a gothically inflected jewellery box – or, more appropriately, an ornate reliquary, as it was built to house holy relics – notably the original crown of thorns worn by Jesus on the cross.

This explains the name given to this modern homage by E. Fay Jones (1921–2004), who wanted to recapture some of Sainte-Chapelle's sense of being enveloped by space and light. It was commissioned by Jim Reed, a retired teacher who hoped that it would be a place of pilgrimage and peace.

TE + DEUM + LAUDAMUS + TE + DOMINUM + CONFITEMUR
FOURNIER
N.ORLEANS

OPPOSITE AND BELOW:
St Louis Cathedral, New Orleans, Louisiana, USA
'You O God we praise; we acknowledge you as Lord…' The words of the *Te Deum* surmount the organ in St Louis Cathedral, on New Orleans's Jackson Square. Dedicated to France's King Louis IX (1214–70) – among other saintly things the builder of Paris's Sainte-Chapelle – this cathedral was founded in 1718, when New Orleans itself was established.

A second, more robust brick and timber structure burned down in the Great Fire of 1788. Its successor was so radically altered by repair and enlargement in the middle of the nineteenth century that it amounted to a third cathedral. This too has been in the wars, in 1909 being damaged by a dynamite blast (an attempted anarchist bombing?) and sustaining damage in several storms – most recently Hurricane Katrina in 2005.

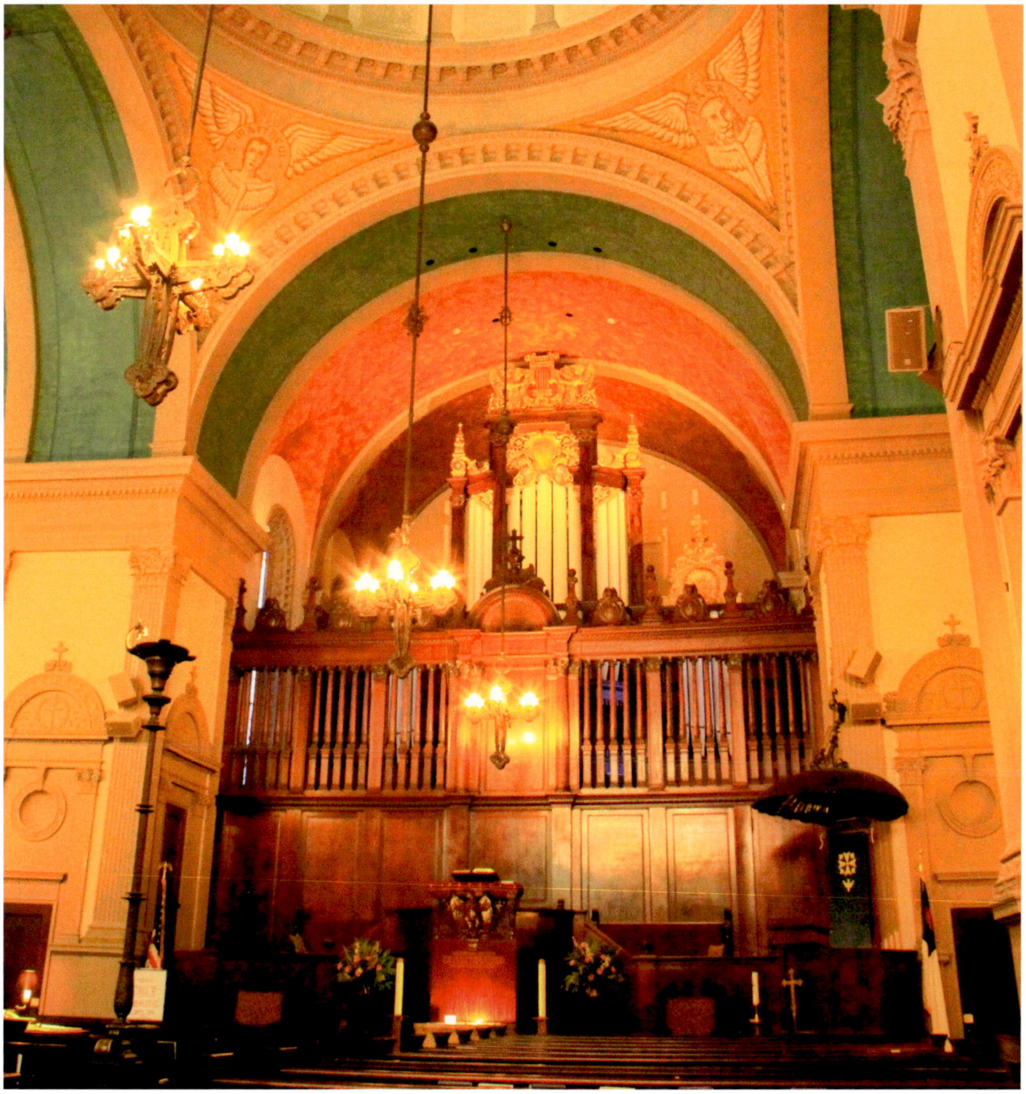

ALL PHOTOGRAPHS:
Memorial Presbyterian Church, St Augustine, Florida, USA
Henry Flagler (1830–1913), founder of Standard Oil and a prime mover in the development of Florida's Atlantic Coast, built this church in 1889 in memory of his daughter Jennie Louise Benedict, who had died at the age of only 34.

Florida's first Presbyterian church, it was modelled on St Mark's Basilica in Venice. This decision was not as whimsical as it may sound. St Augustine's setting, on reclaimed coastal marshland south of Jacksonville, isn't so dissimilar from Venice. No expense was spared: the pews were carved in mahogany, there were beautiful details done in brick and terracotta, the copper dome and marble were shipped in from Italy.

Jennie herself was laid to rest in an adjacent mausoleum. In due time, Henry and other members of the Flagler family would join her there.

Our Lady of Remedies Church, Cholula, Puebla, Mexico
Framed by the smoking cone of Popocatepetl, this historic church stands atop what looks like another mountain but is in fact an ancient pyramid built by the indigenous civilization which once reigned here. The symbolism could hardly be much plainer: the triumph of Christianity over paganism. It's lent still more force by the association between Our Lady of Remedies and the *Reconquista* – the Christian 'reconquest' of Moorish Spain – and the tradition that her image had helped the conquistador Hernán Cortés to victory over the Aztecs in 1520.

ALL PHOTOGRAPHS:
New Basilica of Our Lady of Guadalupe, Mexico City, Mexico
It was here, according to tradition, that one morning in 1531 a local peasant was accosted by a vision of the Virgin Mary. She told Juan Diego Cuauhtlatoatzin that his community needed her and that he should ask his bishop to build a chapel. But Archbishop Juan de Zumárraga was hugely sceptical about Juan's story. He sent the peasant away while he considered it, and didn't act.

In the weeks that followed, Our Lady appeared three further times to Juan, but only when she miraculously cured his dying uncle was Archbishop Zumárraga finally persuaded and the chapel built. It is believed that this place was already sacred to Mexico's indigenous people. That its sanctity should be so dramatically reaffirmed (and in the face of white, official opposition), underlined its significance for Mexico's peasantry.

One basilica was built in 1709. This new one next door, containing Juan Diego's cloak, was added in 1974.

Church of Santa María Tonantzintla, Cholula, Puebla, Mexico
Religious syncretism – the splicing together of different traditions – has been a longstanding feature of Latin American life. The old, pagan ways maintained a palpable if implicit presence in Catholic religious culture, just as here Our Lady took on the traditional associations of the Aztec mother goddess Tonantzin. And her sixteenth-century church, in its broad architectural outline an example of colonial baroque, took on some of the exuberant forms of indigenous folk art.

Central and South America

For the sixteenth-century Spanish cleric Fray Bartolomé de las Casas (c.1484–1566), colonialism was a religious ministry: 'Christ seeks souls not property,' he said. But not as far as his countrymen were concerned. Nor, it might be thought, could his claim have convinced those exposed to the depredations of European colonists in Central and South America. Along with the tens of thousands killed and enslaved, millions died of Old World diseases such as smallpox, against which they had no immunity. However cruel their conversion, though, many of the region's indigenous peoples soon embraced the creed of Christ, accepting the authority of the Catholic clergy, both in New Spain and in Portuguese Brazil.

If the division between these two linguistic and political spheres seems arbitrary, that's because it is. In the early years of the 'Age of Discovery', at a time when they were still the only two imperialist players, Portugal and Spain agreed the Treaty of Tordesillas. Signed in 1494, this divided the world beyond Europe up along a line running north–south 370 leagues west of the Cape Verde Islands, slicing through the easternmost part of South America. In addition to the East Indies, then, Portugal got Brazil, whilst Spain took the remainder of South America. Not until some four centuries later would attempts to carve up Antarctica begin. Even then, so harsh were conditions there that the colonial powers had little choice but to work cooperatively.

OPPOSITE:
São Francisco de Assis, Ouro Preto, Minas Gerais, Brazil
Ouro Preto's very name (the Portuguese for 'Black Gold'), and even more so its former title 'Villa Rica' ('Rich Town'), sum up the historical heritage of this sometime mining centre. Suffice it to say, it's full of treasures like this rococo church by local architect 'Aleijadinho' (Antonio Francisco Lisboa, 1730–1814).

LEFT:

San Juan Bautista de Remedios Church, Remedios, Villa Clara, Cuba

Remedios lies just a few miles inland from the northern coast of Cuba. Rumour has it that its founder, a Spanish noble, kept its existence secret from the Crown to avoid his tax liabilities. An analogous reasoning seems to have applied when, after the present church was built in 1692, its 13 ornate gold altars were concealed from raiding buccaneers by unassuming coats of plain white paint.

OPPOSITE TOP AND BOTTOM:

Basílica Catedral Nuestra Señora de la Altagracia, Salvaleón de Higüey, Dominican Republic

The story goes that in the sixteenth century an image of Our Lady healed a dying child here. The basilica built between 1946 and 1971 to house the picture has now become the Dominican Republic's foremost shrine. It befits in its splendour the traditional 'Queen of Dominicans' Hearts' (the red, white and blue clothing she's depicted in anticipated the colours of the country's flag). But this is also an uncompromising statement of architectural and spiritual modernism. Constructed almost entirely out of concrete, it's imposingly big yet beautifully elegant. Its slender central arch stands 69m (225ft) tall.

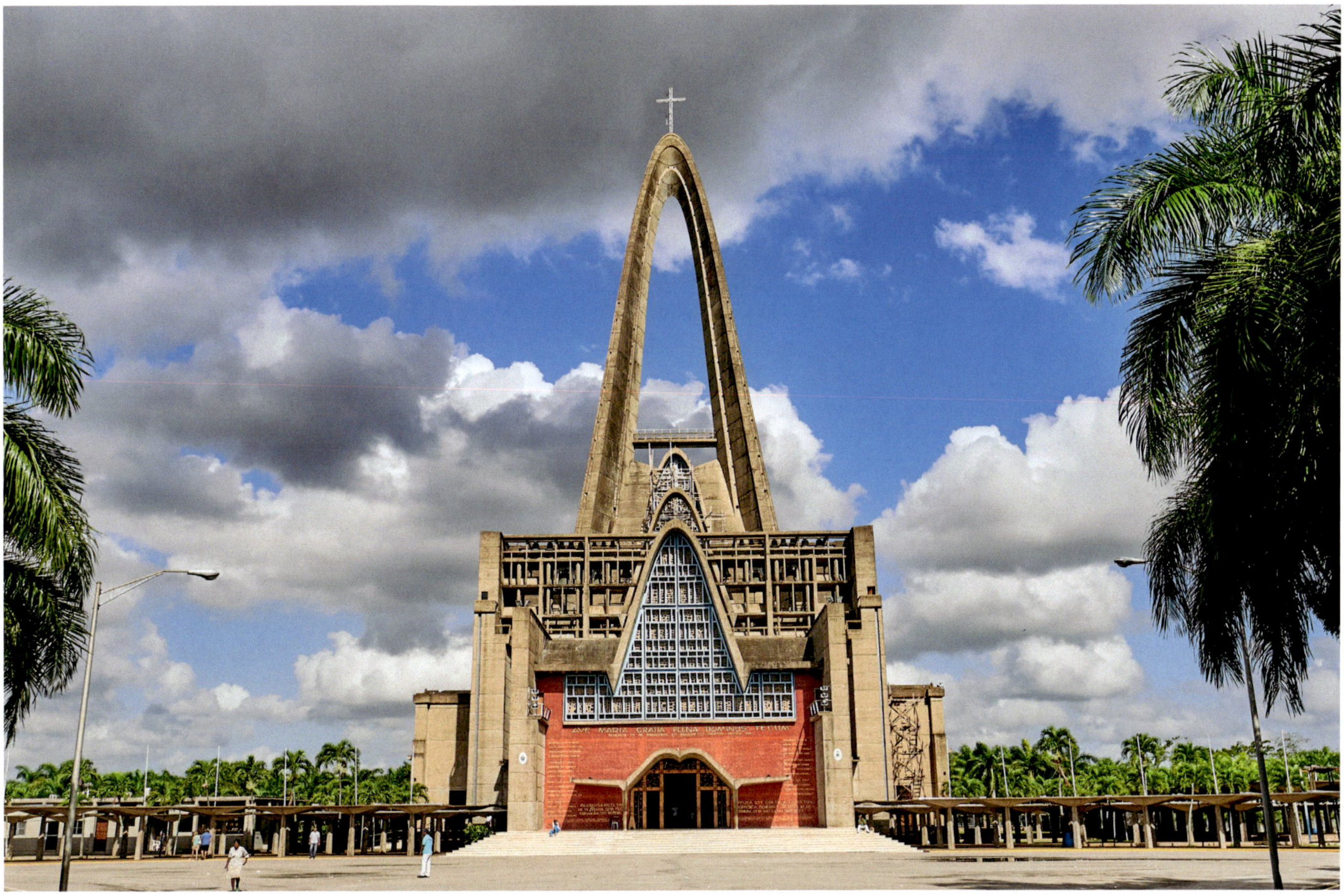

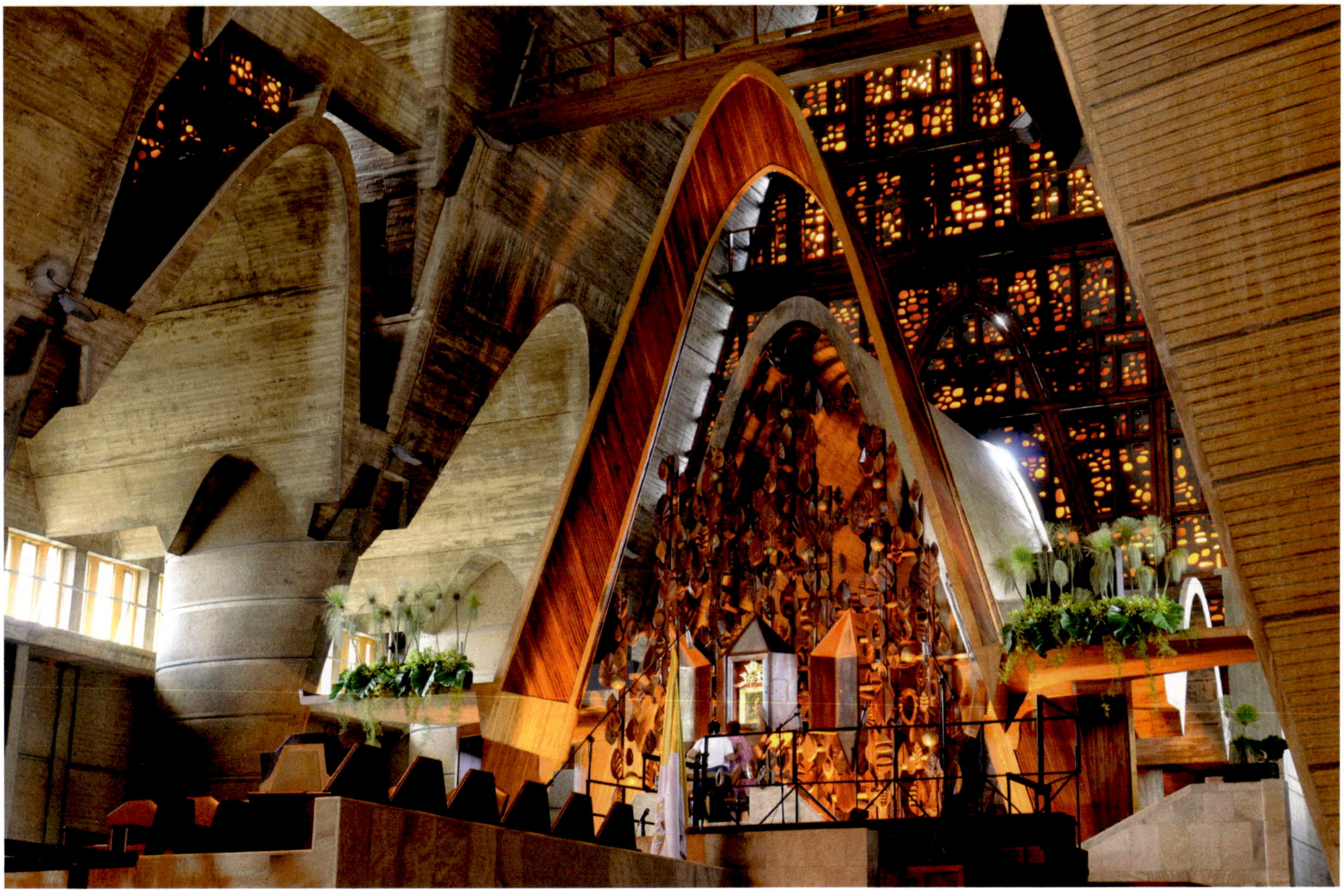

2008
1900
Jesus
Dios Cristo hombre
y
Viue
Reina
ympe
ra
1901

Church of San Andrés Xecul, Totonicapán, Guatemala
Like the Church of Santa María Tonantzintla in Mexico's Cholula, this ebulliently festive-looking church represents the staying power of syncretism – the blending of beliefs – in Latin America's religious culture – specifically, here, the ancestral beliefs and aesthetics of the Maya. Along with saints and acrobatic-looking angels, we see tumbling ferns and winding plants, and even, at the very top, a pair of jaguars.

LEFT:

Las Lajas Sanctuary, Ipiales, Nariño, Colombia

The lajas are the great stone slabs which are such a striking feature of this canyon. It's said that, one dark night in 1754, María Meneses de Quiñones and her deaf-mute daughter, Rosa, were making their way up the valley when a fearful storm broke out. Alarmed at the weather's violence, they sought shelter between two of these stones. As the tempest raged, and they cowered there, María was astonished to hear her little girl find speech. 'The Mestiza [mixed-race lady] is calling me!,' Rosa cried as she pointed upward. There, where the lightning played about the crags, stood the Virgin Mary.

Too stunned to reveal what had happened, mother and daughter resumed their lives, until, a few years later, little Rosa died. At this point, a grief-stricken María returned to this same spot to mourn and offer prayers. Our Lady reappeared, and gave back her living daughter. This time, María told everyone who'd listen. Within weeks a simple wooden chapel had been built here. Over time, as pilgrims came and went, and reports of further healings were heard, this building was gradually improved, and much enlarged.

The church that we see today was constructed between 1916 and 1949, but the image of the Virgin behind the altar dates from the earliest years of the shrine's existence. The faithful believe that it was miraculously created.

ABOVE:
Church El Rosario, San Salvador, El Salvador
San Salvador's Church of the Rosary isn't too much to look at from the outside. It resembles the top of a massive grey glass-and-concrete water wheel. But that only increases the impact of the rainbow-coloured lightshow that the visitor finds inside this church, designed by Salvadoran sculptor Rubén Martínez. It was constructed in 1974 to replace an earlier building that had to be demolished after suffering extensive earthquake damage.

OPPOSITE TOP:
Basilica of Our Lady of the Angels, Cartago, Costa Rica
Another Latin American shrine; another miraculous image of Our Lady – this one a black statue found by a little peasant girl. She thought that it was a doll and took it home. It was gone the next day, but reappeared on the rocks where she'd first found it; she took it back again, and so it went on, and on, over successive days. A clear sign, villagers thought, that a shrine was needed. This modern Byzantine/colonial hybrid dates from 1939.

OPPOSITE BOTTOM:
Immaculate Church of Concepcion de Maria, Liberia, Costa Rica
Liberia acquired the nickname of *Ciudad Blanca* or 'White City' from its wealth of whitewashed houses and its distinctive white-gravel roads. Even if its whiteness is that of unsurpassed innocence and miraculous purity, the Church of the Immaculate Conception of Mary fits right in. Often confused by non-Catholics with the 'virgin birth', the doctrine of Our Lady's immaculate conception refers to her own miraculous conception 'without sin'.

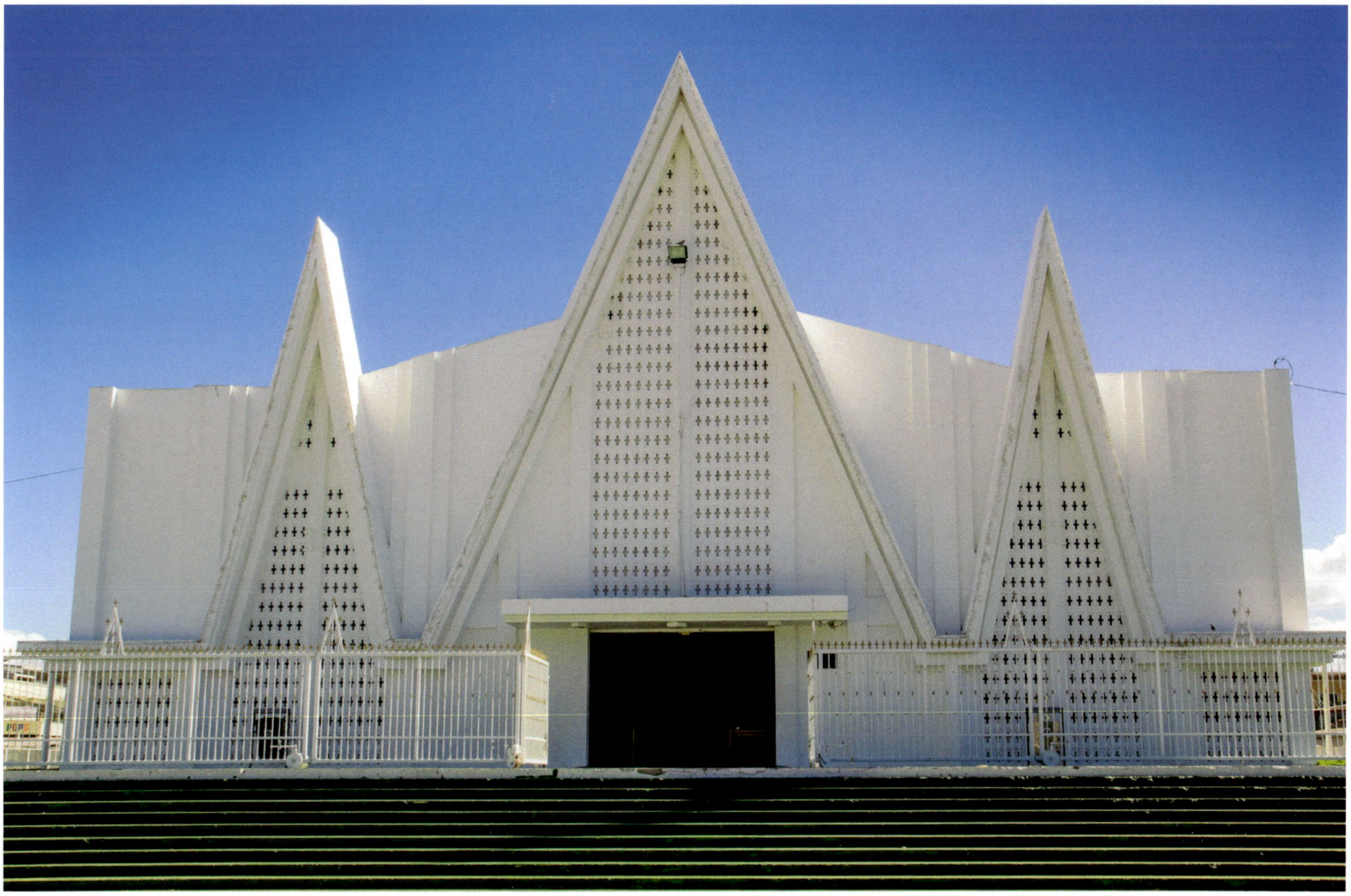

"Vayan donde los blancos,
paraque les echen agua en la cabeza
y asi poder ir al cielo"

12
11
10
9
8
7
6
5
4
3
2

PREVIOUS PAGE:

Basilica of the National Shrine of Our Lady of Coromoto, Portuguesa, Venezuela

Spanish missionaries mounted a strenuous campaign of proselytization in this part of Portuguesa in the 1650s. A local chief, Coromoto, however, led his people in resisting. The Virgin Mary appeared before him and urged him to accept baptism. When he still held out she appeared again. This time he reached out and tried to seize hold of her. She dissolved into thin air, but a picture of her remained. It's preserved inside the church.

LEFT:

Basilica del Voto Nacional, Quito, Ecuador

The 'National Vow' to which this church is dedicated is the legislation that Ecuador's parliament passed in 1871, stating that the whole country should be consecrated to the Sacred Heart of Jesus. A few years later, Gabriel García Moreno (1821–75), the highly conservative president who had led the drive to this decision, was assassinated by revolutionaries.

Work on this great neo-gothic basilica began in 1883, resisted not only by those freethinkers and left-wingers who'd opposed Moreno's measure in the first place, but by the much larger number who resented being taxed for its construction.

St. George's
Cathedral

LEFT AND ABOVE:

St George's Cathedral, Georgetown, Guyana

Guyana's capital got itself a cut-price cathedral in St George's in 1889. A neo-gothic extravaganza: pointed arches, clustered columns, flying buttresses... but all built out of timber. English architect Arthur Blomfield (1829–99) had first suggested a very similar proposal in stone, but the diocese had jibbed at the cost and he'd come back with this design. Making a virtue out of necessity, Blomfield stipulated that, wherever possible, only wood from Guyana itself was to be used. No expense was spared with the stained glass, which shows scenes from the life and death of Christ as well as from the Book of Revelation.

LEFT:
St Peter and Paul Cathedral, Paramaribo, Suriname
This brightly coloured cathedral is believed to be the biggest wooden structure in the Western hemisphere. It was built between 1885 and 1901. The exterior and frame were constructed out of greenheart and basralocus wood, both for their strength and their resistance to insect parasites. The interior is stunning with unpainted cedar panelling and a wealth of wood-carved columns, capitals and other features, all clearly done with exuberant enthusiasm and consummate skill. It's the work of recently freed slaves. The Dutch priests who built St Peter and Paul wanted at once to create employment and to foster a welcome for African-Surinamese people in their church.

LEFT:
Cathedral of Brasilia, Brazil
'I was attracted by the curve – the liberated, sensual curve suggested by the possibilities of new technology yet so often recalled in venerable old baroque churches,' said the architectural genius Oscar Niemeyer (1907–2012), who brought the whole city of Brasilia into being. It's appropriate that he should have been the one to design this house for the ultimate Creator.

NEXT PAGE, TOP LEFT:
Cathedral of Brasilia, Brazil
A leftist and an atheist, Oscar Niemeyer nevertheless respected the religion of his country's poor. The vast stained-glass windows in this cathedral would, he believed, help connect the people to the sky, and their lord's heaven. The church is dedicated to Our Lady of Aparecida, whose celebrated statue has its own shrine outside São Paulo.

NEXT PAGE, BOTTOM LEFT:
Pampulha Church, Pampulha Lake, Minas Gerais, Brazil
'A church is God's hangar on earth,' wrote the French Catholic poet Paul Claudel (1868–1955). The idea was the inspiration for this church, Oscar Niemeyer maintained. God's opinion isn't known, but it didn't find favour with the local clergy – one of whom pronounced Pampulha Church 'unfit for religious purposes'. Times have changed, and with them attitudes: today its aesthetic – and spiritual – worth are at last being appreciated.

NEXT PAGE, BOTTOM RIGHT:
Cathedral of Maringa, Parana, Brazil
Built between 1958 and 1972, and supposedly inspired by the achievements of the USSR's Sputnik programme, the Cathedral of Maringá (full name: Catedral Metropolitana Basílica Nossa Senhora da Glória) does appear almost to be straining upwards towards space. Vaguely rocket-shaped, it rises 124m (407ft) above the centre of Maringá, a newly developed city in the south of Brazil.

RELIQUIA
CRANEO SANTA ROSA DE LIMA

OPPOSITE AND ABOVE:

St Rose of Lima, Peru

The sumptuousness of St Rose's reliquary in the Basilica of Santo Domingo – the saint's sometime convent – starkly sets off the grim greyness of her skull. It's wreathed round the brow with roses. As a girl, Rose had worn such a wreath, to please her mother, but also, underneath it, a crown of thorns. Her Sanctuary (above) was built on the site of the house where she'd been born in 1586. Beautiful and wellborn, Rose had dashed her parents' hopes of a good marriage by embracing the religious life.

ABOVE:
Asunción Cathedral, Paraguay
The cathedral of Paraguay's capital is, inevitably, dedicated to Our Lady of the Assumption – her elevation directly, and physically, to heaven. The first church here was built by the Spanish *conquistadores* in 1539; this one went up in 1845.

OPPOSITE TOP AND BOTTOM:
Church, Puerto Varas, Llanquihue, Chile
This part of southern Chile's 'Lake District' saw a great deal of German immigration in the middle of the nineteenth century, a fact which is reflected in local customs and cuisine – and in the architectural vernacular. Nowhere is this more striking than in Puerto Varas's beautifully painted church – wood-built, but clad in iron sheeting.

Constructed between 1915 and 1918, its design was based on the churches of Baden-Württemberg in southwest Germany, especially Rottenburg Cathedral.

NEXT PAGE:
San Francisco Church, Salta, Argentina
Richly decorated inside and out, this convent church was built between the 1850s and 1860s. It has an imposing barrel-vaulted nave, and, reaching 54m (177ft) high, the tallest church tower in South America.

ABOVE:

Old Church, Angastaco, Salta, San Carlos, Argentina

Its dazzling white walls and yellow-cream trim set off stunningly by a clear blue mountain sky, Angastaco's Old Church stands atop a plinth of stony steps. Despite its (loosely) colonial style, the church dates only from the 1940s.

RIGHT:

Christ Church Cathedral, Port Stanley, Falkland Islands

The whalebone arch went up in 1933 in celebration of a hundred years' rule by the British in the Falkland Islands. Half a century later, in 1982, their dominion was almost ended when the Argentinians invaded what they called 'Las Malvinas'. As for Christ Church, its affiliations could hardly be clearer. This red-brick and stone Anglican church might be on any street corner in any town in England.

BELOW AND OVERLEAF:

Grytviken Church, South Georgia

Built by the Church of Norway in 1913, this little Lutheran chapel was (exactly a century later) transferred to the Anglican diocese of the Falkland Islands. The explorers Ernest Shackleton (1874–1922) and Frank Wild (1873–1939) are among more than 60 people laid to rest in the cemetery across the harbour.

ANNO
1913

Trinity Church, Antarctica

Since 2004, when this Orthodox church was built near Bellingshausen Station, a corner of Antarctica has been forever Russia. It wasn't just built of Siberian pine: it was built of Siberian pine in the Altai Mountains in Siberia, before being carried to Kaliningrad on the Baltic and shipped to its present site. It stands 15m (50ft) tall and can hold congregations of up to 30 people. In 2007, a priest here conducted what is believed to have been the first church wedding in Antarctica: the bride was Russian; her Chilean husband was a convert to the Orthodox Church.

NOVALAND

Asia and the Pacific

On 8 February, 1545, Francis Xavier wrote home to his Jesuit superiors about the satisfaction that he was finding in his missionary work in India: 'I know not how to describe the joy I feel before the spectacle of pulling down and destroying the idols by the very people who formerly worshipped them.'

Fair enough, from his point of view, perhaps, though it has taken Westerners until obscenely recently to see how generally destructive their countries' colonialism (even well-intentioned Christian colonialism) has been. Christianity was always an alien creed across much of Asia and the Pacific; its churches have represented an implanted religious and architectural culture. A suggestion of Chartres or Reims on some Indochinese street corner, a glimpse of the English shires in a New Zealand city centre, a flourish of Spanish baroque in the Philippines.... These are colonial impositions, that's quite clear.

And yet they've been there long enough now to have acquired their own history and heritage; many have a beauty all their own. Whatever the rudeness of its first arrival, Christianity has since then woven itself into the fabric of life in Asia and the Pacific. Some wonderful churches stand in witness to the part it has played.

OPPOSITE:

Notre-Dame Cathedral, Ho Chi Minh City, Vietnam

This great cathedral was simply L'Église de Saigon ('Church of Saigon') when it was originally consecrated in 1880 and the city, still commonly referred to as Saigon, was the capital of French Indochina. In keeping with its colonial status, it was built with materials brought in from France: the beautiful bright red bricks came from Toulouse.

Noravank Monastery, Yeghegnadzor, Armenia
Spectacularly situated in the mountains south of Lake Sevan, the Noravank complex dates back to the fourteenth century. It belongs to the Armenian Apostolic Church, a branch of Eastern Orthodoxy. Dedicated to Surb Ashvatsatsin, the Holy Mother of God, this church was built in 1339. Its designer, Momik, was distinguished as a sculptor as well as for his architecture – and his creation here does look as if it's been carved out of the valley's virgin stone. Reliefs above the doors on the western side, with its converging steps, show the Virgin Mary flanked by the Archangels Michael and Gabriel and Christ, with Saints Peter and Paul.

LEFT:

Tsminda Sameba (Holy Trinity) Church, Gergeti, Georgia

High up on a mountaintop in the Khevi, northeast Georgia, this fourteenth-century foundation belongs to the Georgian Orthodox Church. It is built to a cross-shaped ground plan and is surmounted by a cupola, or dome, rounded on the inside but polygonal without. A separate bell-tower stands off to one side. The church's antique beauty and the sublimity of its setting have made it iconic, and it's long been an important destination, not just for pious pilgrims but for Georgian patriots. Its importance to the country is suggested by the fact that the authorities built a 5.6km (3½ mile) road here up the vertiginous mountainside.

OPPOSITE:

Holy Trinity Cathedral of Tbilisi, Georgia

Its traditional appearance notwithstanding, this great church was built only recently, between 1995 and 2004. Its construction was intended to commemorate the (approximately) 1500th year of the Georgian Orthodox Church's autonomous existence and the 2000th anniversary of the birth of Jesus Christ. Inevitably, if less explicitly, it also marked the emergence of the Georgian nation and its Church from the systematic repression both had suffered under seven decades of Soviet rule, though its construction was to be delayed by several years of civil war in which the Russians backed separatist movements in some parts of Georgia. The cathedral is known locally as Sameba, from the Georgian for 'Trinity'.

OPPOSITE TOP:
Church of the Exaltation of the Holy Cross, Almaty, Kazakhstan
Almost a quarter of Kazakhstan's population are Christians, most belonging to the Eastern Orthodox Church. This imposing church stands in the country's second city. It was completed in 2011.

OPPOSITE BOTTOM:
Catholic Church, Karaganda, Kazakhstan
This church was built to commemorate Kazakh Catholics persecuted during the Soviet era. Not only were the Communists committed atheists: they saw the Church as a rival authority.

ABOVE:
Cathedral of the Sacred Heart of Jesus, Tashkent, Uzbekistan
Begun in 1912, but not completed until 2000, this Catholic cathedral is also known as the 'Polish Church'. This is partly because of the contribution in its construction of Polish POWs (from the Austro-Hungarian army) in World War I. It's also because of the association with the 'Anders' Army' during World War II. Polish general Władysław Anders (1892–1970) led volunteers via the Middle East to Central Asia. From 1942 they were headquartered in Tashkent, before going on to fight in Europe.

LEFT:
Holy Trinity Cathedral, Karakol City, Kyrgyzstan
Kyrgyzstan came under Russian rule in 1869. An Orthodox cathedral, constructed in Karakol three years later, served as a visual symbol of the authority of the Tsar. It was impressively built in stone, but was razed by an earthquake in 1890.

The present structure, consecrated in 1895, is largely made of wood. In 1916, its priests were massacred in unrest leading up to the Bolshevik Revolution. Under Soviet rule it was closed down completely. In the decades that followed, it did service as an education and social centre. It was given back to the Orthodox Church in 1991.

LEFT:
St Patrick's Cathedral, Karachi, Pakistan
Catholic missionaries in nineteenth-century India ministered mostly to Europeans – soldiers and officials – and did little to disrupt relations between, or with, the 'Natives'. Hence the tolerance (and sometimes support) of the British authorities.

ABOVE:
Sacred Heart Cathedral, Lahore, Pakistan
Catholicism was more welcoming than Anglicanism to poor Hindus who hoped to sidestep some of the workings of their society's caste-system. Increasing numbers converted in the nineteenth century. Even so, they were a small minority: today only 1.6 per cent of the population of Pakistan is even Christian. The Catholics of Lahore, however, have this imposing Roman Byzantine-style cathedral. It was built for them by Belgian missionaries and consecrated in 1907.

RIGHT:

Basilica of Bom Jesus, Old Goa, Goa, India

Bom means 'good' in Portuguese, the language of the original colonial settlers here, sailing in the wake of Vasco da Gama's visit to these coasts at the very end of the fifteenth century. These Portuguese merchants and seafarers were followed in their turn by the Spanish Jesuit missionary Francis Xavier (1506–52), who made Goa his headquarters in India. In the years that followed, he travelled extensively in India, making converts. Subsequent expeditions were to take him on to the East Indies, China and Japan. On his death, his remains were laid to rest here.

HI MHOJI KUDD
PLEASE KEEP SILENCE
PLEASE KEEP SILENCE

Basilica of Bom Jesus, Old Goa, Goa, India
Completed in 1605, this basilica, a stunning example of architectural baroque, remains a very important shrine. The missionary Francis Xavier has a special place in the history of both the Asian and the global Church. Events from his life are shown in paintings around the church, while his bones lie in a reliquary endowed by Cosimo III de' Medici (1642–1723), Grand Duke of Tuscany.

HSBC

GARDEN ROAD
花園道
4-8

PREVIOUS PAGE:

St John's Cathedral, Hong Kong, China

This Anglican cathedral dedicated to St John the Evangelist (Gospel-writer) was built in the 1840s during the early years of Britain's presence in Hong Kong. Stylistically, it reflects the gothic-revival values current in the ecclesiastical architecture of that time, although it's comparatively plain and austere in its design. At the heart of Hong Kong's business district, it's dwarfed by the skyscrapers that have since sprung up all around.

LEFT:

Catholic Church of the Saviour, Beijing, China

Xuanye, the Kangxi Emperor (1654–1722), gave a plot of land to the Society of Jesus (Jesuits) to build a 'Saviour Church' in 1694. In the 1880s, though, the land was needed for the expansion of Beijing's Forbidden City. The original church was demolished and this one was built as a replacement.

In 1900, during the anti-Western 'Boxer Rebellion', the priests took refuge here with several thousand Chinese congregants. They were subjected to a two-month siege. Finally, the rebels stormed the church: it's said that 400 men, women and children were massacred.

여 의 도
YOIDO FUL

복 음 교 회
GOSPEL CHURCH

PREVIOUS PAGE:
Yoido Full Gospel Church, Seoul, South Korea
Health and wealth are as much part of God's plan for his believers as spiritual salvation, says the Pentecostal Gospel. This church first opened its doors in 1958. Its founder, David Yonggi Cho, was to build up a worldwide congregation more than three-quarters of a million strong, with missionaries in more than 60 countries.

OPPOSITE:
St Mary's Cathedral, Tokyo, Japan
An earlier, wood-built gothic Catholic cathedral went up in flames – along with most of metropolitan Tokyo – in one of a succession of US air raids during World War II. This ultra-modern-looking church was accordingly built alongside a whole new ultra-modern-looking city. Completed in 1964, its exterior is slick and silver-shiny, its interior dark and rough in texture with eight hyperbolic parabolas converging in a cross. 'I began to imagine new spaces,' said Kenzo Tange, the cathedral's architect, 'and I wanted to create them using modern technology.'

ABOVE:
High-Heel Wedding Church, Budai Township, Chiayi County, Taiwan, China
This 17m (56ft) shoe in glass and concrete caters to young couples in Budai Township. It's apparently the biggest high-heel-shaped building in the world.

LEFT AND ABOVE:

Cathedral of the Sacred Heart of Jesus, Tan Dinh, Ho Chi Minh City, Vietnam

Like Ho Chi Minh City's (Saigon's) Notre-Dame Cathedral, the Tan Dinh Church is a product of the colonial period. Founded by French missionary Father Donatien Éveillard (1835–83), it was consecrated in 1876. Éveillard died a few years later and was buried in the church that he'd built, but within a few years of that Sacred Heart was crumbling around his grave. It was pulled down and a new structure – a tall and shapely church in the neo-gothic style, with certain Romanesque and Renaissance features – was sited on the same foundations.

Fast-forward half a century or so and the 'new' church was getting tired and shabby in its turn. Extensive refurbishments were carried out in the 1950s. It seems to have been in 1957 that the decision was taken to paint the exterior salmon pink, with a brighter, fondant pink alternating with bright icing-white within the nave. Some of the same 'camp' quality is to be found in the decoration of the chapels. Astonishingly enough, it never quite seems vulgar.

SILENCE

PREVIOUS PAGE:

St Mary's Cathedral, Yangon, Myanmar

Built in the 1890s, this redbrick gothic-revival church has a bright and bold and even cheerful air. Inside, we see, the décor is still more striking. The city of Yangon stands on reclaimed land on a river delta. The cathedral site was soft and marshy so hardwood piles had to be driven deep into the earth to increase support.

LEFT:

Santa Cruz Church, Bangkok, Thailand

This lovely Renaissance-revival church in Kudi Chin district on the banks of the Chao Praya River was built between 1913 and 1916. Its foundation goes back further, though, to the 1770s, when Portuguese Catholic missionaries set up a headquarters here on land granted to them by King Taksin the Great (1734–82). Taksin was a warlike ruler, but also an eager Westernizer, encouraging commercial and cultural contact with the European countries.

IHS
CATHOLIC CHURCH
CHONG KHNIES

OPPOSITE:

Catholic Church, Komprongpok, Tonlé Sap Lake, Cambodia

Something like a million people live in the various floating villages scattered along the shores of Tonlé Sap in the Mekong Basin. They fish in the lake's waters and grow rice along its swampy margins. Otherwise, they lead normal lives – albeit on the water. Not just their homes, but their schools and churches are built on rafts.

TOP RIGHT:

Christ Church, Malacca, Malaysia

The Dutch took Malacca from the Portuguese in 1541 and helped themselves to Our Lady's Catholic Church. That building still stands, though in a semi-ruined state. In 1753, they built their own new Protestant church in brick and plaster (originally white). It passed from the Dutch Reform to the Anglican communion when Britain's East India Company took over the colony in 1824.

BOTTOM RIGHT:

Abandoned Church, Bokor National Park, Kampot, Cambodia

Standing 1048m (almost 3500ft) above sea-level, southern Cambodia's Bokor Mountain summit offers some relief from the tropical heat. Hence its development by the French colonialists of the nineteenth century as a 'hill station' – a place they could escape to from their sweaty, sultry city of Phnom Penh. This Catholic church offered a spiritual centre for what was, until the 1940s, a bustling resort.

ABOVE:
St Therese Cathedral, Savannakhet, Laos
Laos is justly famous for its French colonial architecture: this dates from the time when the country was part of French Indochina, between the 1890s and the early 1950s. St Therese's is a 'co-cathedral' in the sense that Laotian Catholicism has another 'mother church' in St Louis' in Thakhek.

RIGHT:
St Thomas of Villanueva Church, Miag-ao, Iloilo, Philippines
Built by the Spanish in the eighteenth century, this church has primarily been celebrated for the sumptuously sculpted baroque façade which covers what is essentially a massive, Romanesque structure underneath. Its interior is easily overlooked, then, though it's very beautiful and atmospheric.

ABOVE:

St Andrew's Cathedral, Singapore

The presence of a large and munificent Caledonian contingent among the colonial British population in the 1830s ensured the naming of Singapore's main Anglican church after Scotland's patron saint. That building, just about universally agreed to be ugly and impractical, was (perhaps fortunately) damaged by lightning strikes and had to be demolished and replaced.

The present building was completed in 1861 (it was consecrated as a cathedral nine years later). Its architect is believed to have been inspired by Netley Abbey, a ruined thirteenth-century Cistercian monastery in Hampshire, England. St Andrew's neo-gothic construction (finished outside with Chennai-style chunam or lime-plaster) is certainly consistent with this theory. The resemblance is most obvious in the arches within the nave. St Andrew's is striking in its shimmering white interior, which sets off some fine stained glass to great advantage.

RIGHT:

St Alphonsus Church, Singapore

This church became known informally as the 'Novena Church' after the nine-day prayer-cycle offered there. After that, even the district around it became known as the 'Novena'. A handsome building with an old-world atmosphere, it was, in fact, only built in 1950.

OPPOSITE:

Graha Maria Annai Velangkanni, Medan, Indonesia

Not a Buddhist temple or a Mughal mosque but a Catholic church – a Marian shrine, indeed. In Velangkanni, Tamil Nadu, India, in the seventeenth century, 'Our Lady of Good Health' appeared to a shepherd boy, after which a number of miraculous cures were worked. Her statue, sent to Indonesia in 2002, has been associated with further healings at what has since become an important place of pilgrimage.

ALLAH BERSABDA
JADILAH
AULA SANTA ANNA

RIGHT:

St Mary's Cathedral, Sydney, New South Wales, Australia

Architect Edmund Blacket (1817–83) came to this project directly from his work on Sydney's other, Anglican, cathedral – St Andrew's. Built in the 'perpendicular' (high and extravagantly vaulted) gothic style, that church might be seen as a dry-run for this larger, more ambitious work. Although St Mary's was started in 1868 and in use from 1882, it wasn't finally completed until 2000.

OPPOSITE TOP:

Anglican Cathedral, Darwin, Northern Territory, Australia

The original cathedral on this site was only built in 1902, but was left substantially in ruins by Cyclone Tracy in December 1974. Of all the devastation caused by the storm in Darwin, the damage here was arguably a blessing in disguise. The old cathedral had been a boring barn of a church. Elements of it – the front wall and portico – were cunningly incorporated into the new cathedral, an unabashedly modern one completed in 1977.

OPPOSITE BOTTOM:

Floating Wedding Chapel, Brisbane, Queensland, Australia

For the perfect nautical nuptials, this little chapel offers everything – pulpit, pews, stained glass … and all afloat!

OVERLEAF:

Cardboard Cathedral, Christchurch, New Zealand

In principle an interim arrangement, though it's been here since 2013, Christchurch's pro-cathedral stands in for the wrecked real thing. Not only does it serve as a church, it memorializes the devastation and loss of life caused by the 2011 earthquake. And provides a present monument to the indomitable spirit of Christchurch and its people's determination to struggle on.

Hanga Roa, Easter Island
This stunningly decorated Catholic church is a triumphant expression of syncretism, incorporating as it does both indigenous and Western elements.

The Middle East and Africa

Christ's prophecy that 'the last will be first, and the first last' (Matthew 20, 16) is being fulfilled in an unexpected way. With birth rates faltering in Europe and in North America, and church attendance falling still more steeply, what were once the 'peripheries' of Christianity are now coming to the fore. Africa isn't just the Church's future, Pope Francis told young people in Maputo, Mozambique, in 2019. Africa's Christians are its *present* – and getting more important every day.

Christianity's 'first' place chronologically will always belong to the Middle East, of course. The 'Holy Places' of the Gospels are here, attracting pilgrims in their millions. Nor is there any obvious likelihood of this changing. Beyond these sacred precincts, though, the churches are under pressure, caught between the rise in secularism and, in some places, an increasingly militant Islam.

Such developments only make the role of Africa that much more decisive. Its people won't just be passive recipients of the Gospel message. Time was – and very recently – when Christian missions saw themselves as bringing light to the 'Dark Continent', civilization to the 'savage'. That thinking is not just wrong: it's inadequate to our times. Africa seems likely to change the Church every bit as much as the Church is likely to change Africa.

OPPOSITE:
Church of the Holy Sepulchre, Jerusalem, Israel
Omniscient God, the all-seeing eye, and his son Jesus, light of the world, are both emblematized in the 'oculus' in the dome of this church. In its hallowed spaces, pilgrims have for centuries felt the presence of the Holy Spirit, transporting their emotions and reinvigorating their faith.

ALL PHOTOGRAPHS:

Church of the Holy Sepulchre, Jerusalem, Israel

No shrine could be more sacred than this. The Holy Sepulchre encompasses not just the summit of Mount Calvary, where Christ was crucified, but the tomb in which his tortured corpse was laid. His Resurrection on the third day was, of course, to be the founding miracle of the Christian faith, so the church is naturally a magnet for pilgrims.

There's a whole complex of buildings here, including a beautifully decorated Coptic chapel (opposite) and, on the roof, the Deir es-Sultan monastery, plus the twelfth-century Armenian Chapel of St Helena (above).

Ο ΕΥΑΓΓΕΛΙΣΤΗΣ ΜΑΡΚΟΣ
Ο ΕΥΑΓΓΕΛΙΣΤΗΣ ΛΟΥΚΑΣ
IC XC
Ο ΕΥΑΓΓΕΛΙΣΤΗΣ ΜΑΤΘΑΙΟΣ
Ο ΕΥΑΓΓΕΛΙΣΤΗΣ ΙΩΑΝΝΗΣ

Church of the Annunciation, Nazareth, Israel
'The Angel of the Lord declared unto Mary … And the Word was made flesh, and dwelt amongst us.' The inscription commemorates the Archangel Gabriel's announcement to Mary that, though a virgin, she was to be the mother of God's son. This basilica is built on the reputed site of Our Lady's home. The actual 'Holy House' was transported to Loreto, Italy, where it has been a place of pilgrimage since the fourteenth century.

NVNTIAVIT MARIAE
S. LVCAS
S. JOANNES
ET HABITAVIT IN NOBIS
NOMEN

St George Greek Orthodox Cathedral, Beirut, Lebanon
Since the fifth century, a series of cathedrals here have had to be razed and rebuilt because of earthquakes. This eighteenth-century successor was all but destroyed in the Civil War of 1975–90. The conflict wasn't straightforwardly sectarian: most of its so-called 'Christian militias' were Maronites, ultimately affiliated to the Catholic Church, but so grand a cathedral was inevitably a target. Restoration has been under way in recent years.

ABOVE:
St Anthony of Padua Church, Istanbul, Turkey
The neo-Venetian style – and St Anthony's patronage – reflect the largely Italian congregation of this lovely little church in the district of Beyoglu on the European side of Istanbul. This area was historically the hub for trade with Genoa and Venice.

OPPOSITE AND LEFT:
Church of St George, Madaba, Jordan
This church is justly celebrated for its floor, which boasts a Byzantine mosaic map of sixth-century Jerusalem and the city's holy places, but it's well worth raising your eyes to look around more generally. The church's spiritual function apart, this is an earthly treasure house, packed with beautiful artworks of every kind, from carpets to icons, from wood-carved furniture to altarware.

Churches of Göreme, Cappadocia, Turkey
Who needs domes or spires? The Göreme Valley gets its otherworldly appearance from the effects of millions of years of erosion on a landscape of compacted volcanic ash or 'tuff'. For centuries, hillsides here have been hollowed out to make space for some of the world's most striking – and eerily atmospheric – churches, their rock walls richly painted or carved with crosses.

OPPOSITE AND ABOVE:
Churches of Göreme, Cappadocia, Turkey
With angels attending him on every side and saints and apostles lined up at his feet, Christ sits enthroned in this stunning fresco at Hacli Kilise (above). Like many such Byzantine paintings, it exploits the vaulting's curvature to provide perspective and a sense of depth.

Figurative art would have been widely frowned upon by the area's Muslim inhabitants – but also by Orthodox Christians themselves during periods of 'iconoclastic' puritanism. Either of those might explain the obliteration of the faces here. The Christians' 'all-seeing eye' at bottom centre would readily have been confused with the 'evil eye' of popular superstition, so it's easy enough to see why that would have been destroyed.

The walls in this arched recess (opposite) have been left blank, but a scene with saints and angels guard the entrance from above.

RIGHT:

Virgin Mary and St Simon the Tanner Cathedral, Cairo, Egypt

Simon the Tanner, a tenth-century Coptic saint, is best known for the story that he literally moved a mountain to demonstrate God's power to a doubtful caliph. Here, that feat seems to have struck some sort of analogous chord with Christ's Resurrection and the rolling aside of the stone that stood outside the Saviour's tomb. St Simon's Church has been carved out of Cairo's Mokattam Mountain, the exact feature that he is said to have moved.

There was a cave here before (discovered in 1974), but whilst it extended deep beneath the rock and stretched over a wide area, it was full to the roof with stones and had only a metre's (3ft) gap at its main entrance. Work began to open up and clear the cavern to create this cathedral in 1991.

OVERLEAF:

Archangel Michael's Coptic Orthodox Cathedral, Aswan, Egypt

Supposedly started by St Mark, Egypt's Coptic Christianity has been marked out from other demoninations in its insistence that the Saviour's human and divine natures were distinct and didn't mingle. To the outsider, this may sound like the 'narcissism of small differences'. But, what can we say? To the committed (on either side), the difference isn't 'small'. This beautiful cathedral was opened in 2006.

إن قلبي ليس فيه
أنا لا أملك هذا الثوب بل
لا أدعيه هو من مالك أنت لك
أن تسترجعيه
قداسة البابا
شنودة الثالث

OPPOSITE AND ABOVE:
Hanging Church, Cairo, Egypt
St Virgin Mary's Orthodox Coptic Church is believed to have been built towards the end of the seventh century above a gatehouse in what had originally been a Roman fortress. The gradual building up of the ground around the church over many centuries of construction, demolition and reconstruction – 6m (20ft) or so in all, archaeologists believe – has, to a considerable extent, cancelled out the impact of its raised situation. Even so, this is an extremely striking church.

Although, nominally, the Coptic Church has always had its headquarters in Alexandria, Cairo's growing importance as Egypt's capital has seen St Virgin Mary's becoming the Church's de facto centre.

Cathédrale du Sacré-Cœur d'Alger, Algiers, Algeria
Could a cathedral look any less inviting? A jagged row of concrete prisms run like shards of broken glass along a wall; what might be the cooling tower for a power station rises above. Inside Sacré-Coeur, which was completed in 1958, though, it's another story. Sunshine streams down through the central tower from what appears to be an all-seeing eye, flooding an open, airy interior with God's light.

PREVIOUS PAGES:
Cathédrale du Sacré-Cœur d'Alger, Algiers, Algeria
Glass-and-concrete forms recall the verse 'The Lord has pitched his tent amongst us' (John 1, 14). Co-designers Paul Herbé (1903–63) and Jean Le Couteur (1916–2010) evidently enjoyed the challenge of fashioning solid, massy concrete into light, thin canvas: an architectural analogy for the mystery of faith.

OPPOSITE AND ABOVE:
Casablanca Cathedral, Morocco
What's in a neo-gothic name? Designed by the French architect Paul Tournon (1881–1964), the Église de Sacré-Coeur, commonly known as Casablanca Cathedral, is generally characterized as being neo-gothic. And so, in a highly stylized way, it is, with skeletal spires and spiked flying buttresses – though it's the neo-gothic viewed through a prism of Art Deco.

But there's a Moroccan influence, too, as exemplified especially by the interior décor, such as the spangling of stained glass inside both towers.

Despite its name, this extraordinary church never actually was a cathedral. Since Moroccan independence in 1956, indeed, it hasn't even been a church. However, as a sort of civic centre, it still fulfils a part of its old role in providing an uplifting monument and a public exhibition space.

NOTRE - DAME - D'AFRIQUE PRIEZ POUR NOUS ET POUR LES MUSUL

LEFT AND BELOW:

Notre-Dame d'Afrique, Algiers, Algeria

This imposing basilica was built about a century before Algiers's Cathédrale du Sacré-Cœur and couldn't be more different aesthetically or, by implication, doctrinally. It was constructed at the instigation of Charles Lavigerie (1825–92) – honoured in the statue below – who was famous for his bid to build French influence in North Africa through preaching Catholicism.

The church is intended to impress, even to cow. The inscription behind the altar reads: *Notre Dame d'Afrique, Priez Pour Nous et Pour Les Musulmanes* ('Our Lady of Africa: Pray for Us and For the Muslims').

OVERLEAF:

Our Lady of Peace, Yamoussoukro, Ivory Coast

'My kingdom is not of this world,' warned Jesus (John 18, 36), though even his own Church has sometimes struggled to remember this. All the great churches in this book are – by some definitions – 'vanity projects'. But surely none more so than Ivorian President Houphouët-Boigny's opulent monument to himself. Pope John Paul II agreed to consecrate it in 1990, but only on condition that a hospital was built nearby.

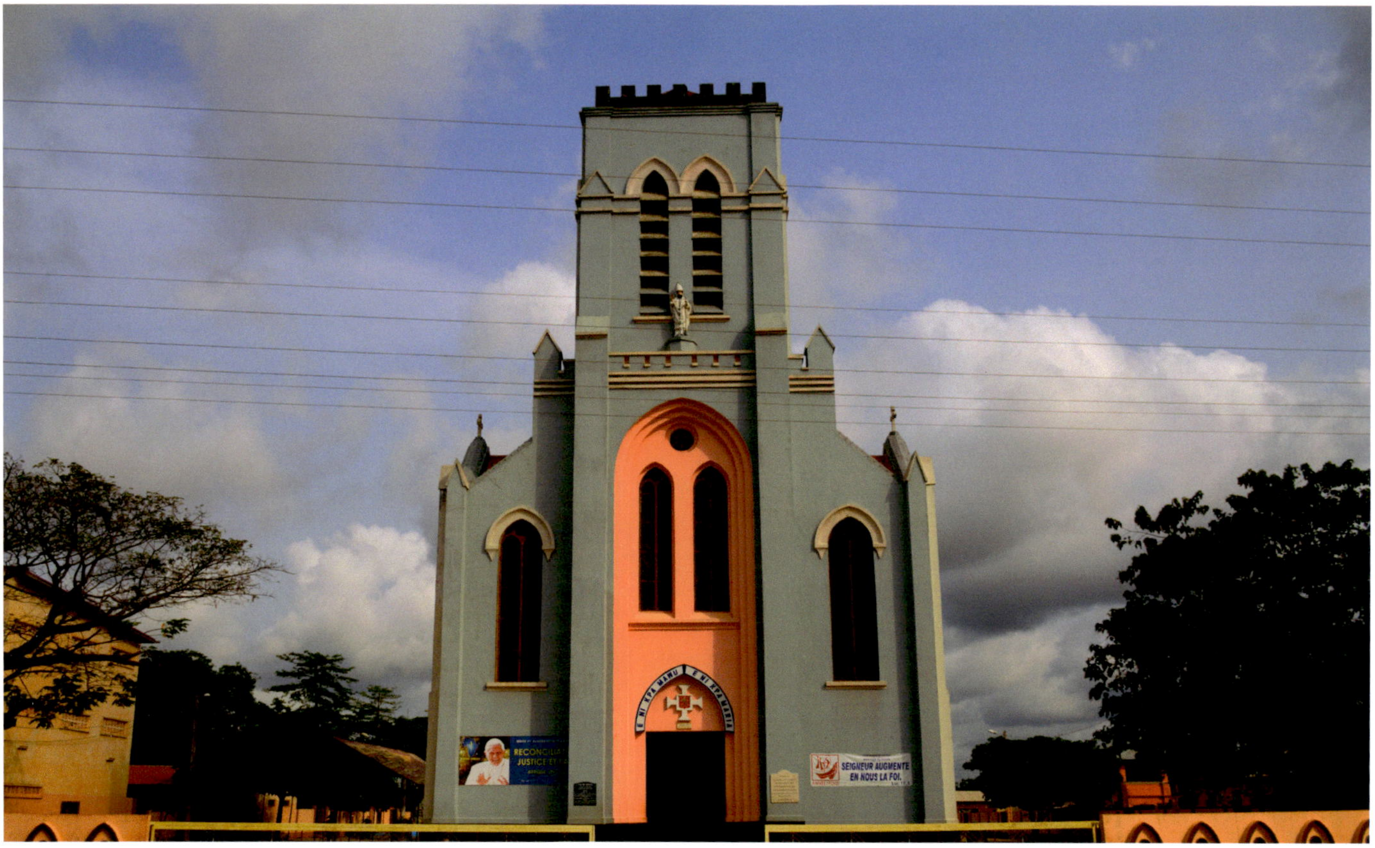

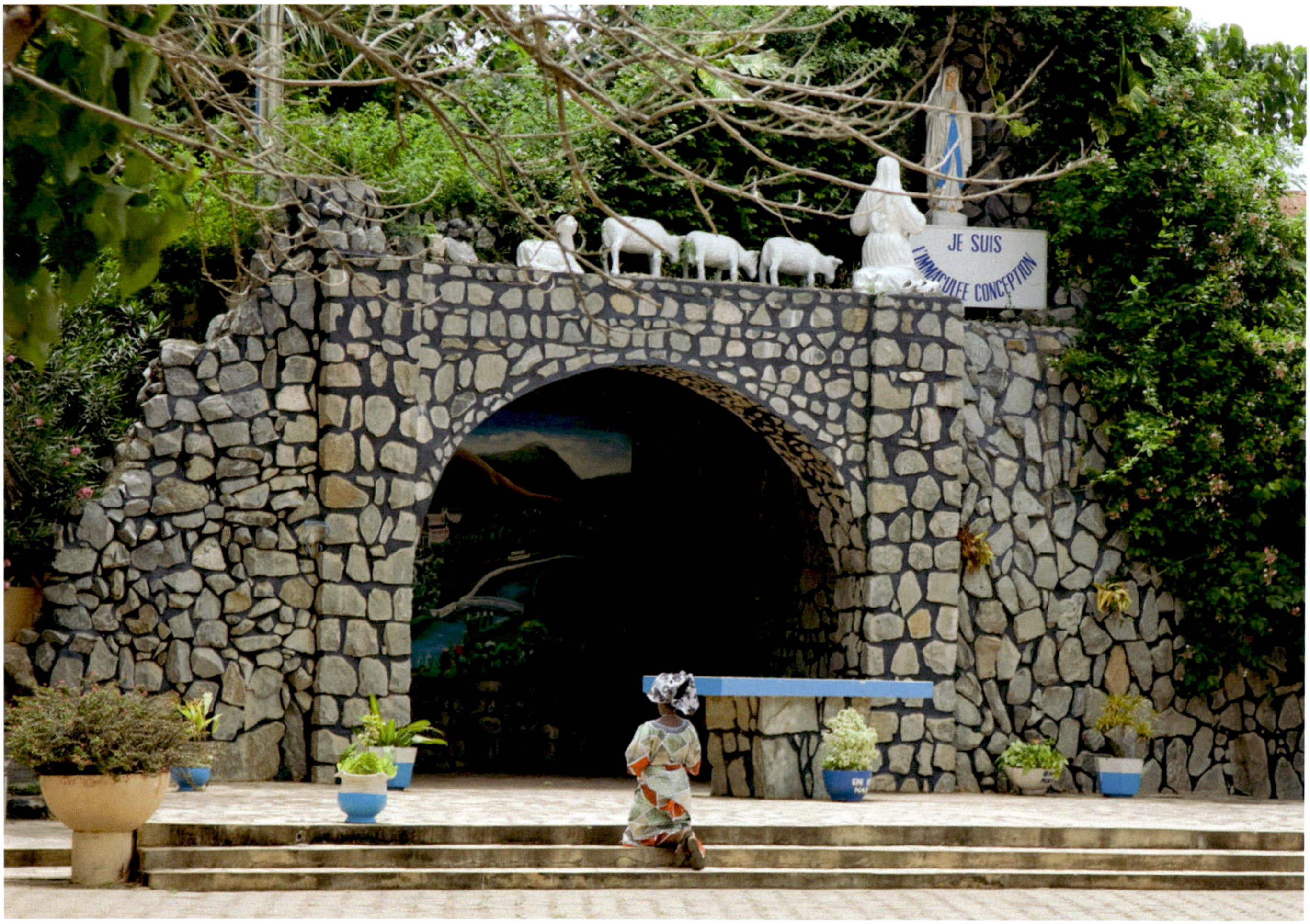

OPPOSITE TOP:
French Church, Ouidah, Benin
This little basilica, consecrated in 1989, is dedicated to the Immaculate Conception of Our Lady.

OPPOSITE BOTTOM:
Catholic Basilica, Ouidah, Benin
'I am the immaculate conception,' Our Lady tells the kneeling figure of St Bernadette (1844–79) above an arched side-entrance to Benin's main basilica.

LEFT:
National Christian Centre, Abuja, Nigeria
Africa is reinventing Christianity – and, it appears, ecclesiastical architecture. This interdenominational church takes neo-gothicism to wild extremes.

BELOW:
Church near Malanje, Angola
Now no more than a shell, this church's state of dereliction reflects the hard times so widely experienced in Angola since the Civil War (1975–2002).

Portuguese Church, Namibe Province, Angola
Catholicism has endured in Angola since the Portuguese colonists were driven out in 1975. Even so, a great many churches stand abandoned, such as this one in the country's south-eastern desert.

HIC · DOMVS · DEI

OPPOSITE:

Church, Baia Dos Tigres, Angola

'This is the house of God,' says the inscription, though there's no obvious sign that anyone's at home. Angola's empty churches don't indicate a collapse of faith following the departure of the Portuguese, but the legacy of the ensuing 25-year Civil War, which left wide areas devastated.

BELOW:

Lubango Cathedral, Angola

Fernando Batalha (1908–2012) built this monument in 'modernized gothic' in 1939. Like Paul Tournon's Casablanca Cathedral, it shows clear (if understated) Art Deco influence.

Church, Sikaunzwe, Kazungula, Zambia
Long after Sub-Saharan Africa had been converted, the Christian missions still had work to do, running schools, colleges, hospitals and, yes, churches.

Mud construction may be 'primitive' but, done properly, it's a highly practical way of using the most immediately and cheaply available materials to build strong and resilient, naturally insulated homes – and churches.

RIGHT:

Dutch Reformed Church, Greyton, Western Cape, South Africa

As its name suggests, the Dutch Reformed Church was brought to South Africa from the Netherlands by the Afrikaner colonists who settled around the Cape in the seventeenth century. This church is architecturally ambiguous: its needle-like spire, with Art Deco features, contrasts strongly with the rounded lines of the 'Cape Vernacular' architecture that the area is famed for, though the whitewashed walls fit right in with the local style.

OVERLEAF:

Maputo Cathedral, Mozambique

A civil engineer moonlighting as an architect, Marcial Simões de Freitas (1891–1944) made a virtue of necessity when he built this church. Chaste, modest, understated, demure… these are all characteristics we'd associate with saintly maidenhood. They're just as appropriate to a cathedral-building project without funds. Outside, then, a narrow spire, striking in cleanly-whitewashed concrete and cement. Within, a scene of well-nigh Protestant sobriety and restraint.

MISSION OF TABERNACLE OF GLORY
MTGM
SUNDAY SERVICES
1st Service - 9:00am - 10:00am
2nd Service - 10:00am - 1:00pm
Evening - 5:00pm - 7:00pm & Ladies - 3:30pm - 5:00pm
All are welcome to Jesus Solution Centre
MINISTERING
Pst. & Mrs. Alfred Juma
WEEKLY
Wed. 5:30pm - 7:00pm -
Friday Prayers - 5:30pm -
Kesha (Third Friday of
FOR PRAYERS & COUNSELLING:
MISSION: Declaring God's Glory among the

Pentecostal Church, Kamere Township, Nakuru, Kenya
It's no Notre-Dame maybe, but Jesus wouldn't have sneered to see this tin-shack gospel church. In a Kenya where political and economic instability has left large numbers feeling marginalized, traditional Christian forms have failed to meet the people's needs.

Conventional churches have proven rigid, emotionally anaemic and unresponsive to the most urgent, worldly needs of the individual – for a happy marriage, a child, a job, a car. Above all, perhaps, they are patriarchal. Pentecostalism, in contrast, may be socially conservative, but it gives women acknowledgement and a voice.

DOMINO
GLORIA IN EXCELSIS DEO
IHS
IHS

LEFT AND ABOVE:
Mai Mahiu Catholic Church, Kenya
During World War II, Italian prisoners of war were brought to camps in Kenya, and set to work by the British colonial authorities there. One group was employed building a road up the Rift Valley – arduous, difficult and dangerous toil. Despite their exhaustion, they jumped at the opportunity to build themselves their own church – Catholic, of course; the local Anglican churches weren't for them. Architecturally idiosyncratic, their church's quirkiness reflects its construction by amateurs, with vastly more enthusiasm than expertise. Even so, this is a lovely building – peaceful within and picturesque without. 'Come to me my people,' runs the Latin inscription along the top of one wall. 'This is the victory that has won the world by our faith,' says the one along the other.

ABOVE AND OPPOSITE:
Church of St George, Lalibela, Ethiopia
A simple cross cut out of the ground, its level roof flush with the surrounding hillside, St George's stands approximately 30m (98ft) tall. It wasn't 'built' at all in the normal sense: its constructors excavated an enormous trench around a central core from which they then whittled a fully formed church with a beautiful interior. Solid as it is, the church has an almost palpable air of mystery – only when you're up close can you even see that it's there.

It's assumed that Christianity came to Ethiopia as part of the general economic and cultural commerce up and down the Red Sea in about the fourth century, though local legends tell of earlier ministries by Christ's apostles.

High up in the hills of Amhara in northern Ethiopia, Lalibela is said by tradition to have been built at the end of the twelfth century by a saintly king who saw it as a spiritual re-creation of Jerusalem, to which he had recently journeyed as a pilgrim.

Picture Credits

Alamy: 6 (South America), 10/11 (SFL Travel), 13 top (Paul Weston), 13 bottom (Ian Dagnall), 14 top (Paul Cox), 14 bottom (David Forster), 15 top (Ian Dagnall), 23 (Mauritius Images/Steve Vidler), 28 (Imageimage), 29 top left (Travelshots/Peter Phipp), 29 bottom left and right (Hemis/Philippe Blanchot), 48 bottom (Matus Korman), 50 (Timothy Mulholland), 51 top (Bildagentur-online/Exss), 52 (Zoltan Bagosi), 58 (Shaun Ramsay), 60 (PSL Images), 64/65 (Tetra Images/Henryk Sadura), 76 (George Ostertag), 77 (Christoph Rueegg), 83 top (Bildagentur-online/Schickert), 83 bottom (Robert Harding/Richard Cummins), 86 (Maria Janicki), 90 (Inge Johnsson), 91 bottom left (Witold Skrypczak), 95 bottom (Pat & Chuck Blackley), 96/97 (Prisma by Dukas Pressagentur/Raga Jose Fuste), 104 (Age Fotostock), 105 bottom (Hemis/Richard Soberka), 106/107 (Fabrizio Cortesi), 112/113 (Age Fotostock/Jose Enrique Molina), 122 bottom (Travel Pix), 124 (Age Fotostock/Tono Labra), 131 bottom (Cindy Hopkins), 133 (David Lichtneker), 146/147 (Robert Harding/Luca Tettoni), 148/149 (David Parker), 180/181 (Independent Picture Service/Todd Strand), 182/183 (Lucas Vallecillos), 187 (Stefano Politi Markovina), 192/193 (Theodore Liasi), 198/199 (Ivan Vdovin), 200 (Ivan Vdovin), 201 (Design Pics/Axiom/Ian Cumming), 202 (Image Broker/Michael Runkel), 206 bottom (Irene Abdou), 210 (Greaststock/Horst Klemm), 218/219 (Mark Boulton), 220 & 221 (RZAF Images)

Dreamstime: 20 (Lance Brothers), 39 (Alika Obrazovskaya), 47 (Xavier Ambrosioni), 48 top (Frederico Fernandez), 54/55 (Kzysztof Nahlik), 67 (Tneorg), 82 (Coralimages2020), 111 bottom (Pablo Hidalgo), 117 (Matyas Rehak), 120/121 (Rodrigo M Nunes), 122 top (Dabldy), 127 top (Marcelo Vildosola Garrigo), 127 bottom (Matyas Rehak), 128/129 (Diego Grandi), 130 (Antonella 865), 139 (Koba Samurkasov), 164 (Elena Frolova), 165 bottom (Dinozzaver), 168 bottom (Serene Law), 176 (Ra1944), 178 bottom (Vadim Lerner), 179 (Hugoht), 184 (Natalia Volkova), 188 (Byelikova), 194 (Baloncici), 196/197 (Oguz Dikbakan), 208/209 (Andre Silva Pinto), 211 (Kent0344), 214/215 (Grobler du Preez)

Getty Images: 17 (Universal Images Group/Eye Ubiquitous), 40/41 (Crbis/VCG/Atlantide Photography), 66 bottom (Photodisc/Medio Images), 70/71 (E+/traveler1116), 72 (Photographer's Choice/Bruce Leighty), 78/79 & 80/81 (Lonely Planet Images/Pete Unger), 92 (Lonely Planet Images/Richard Cummins), 102 (Corbis/Atlantide Phototravel), 125 (Hulton/Heritage Images), 126 (Image Bank/Luis Castaneda Inc.), 136/137 (Moment/Tigran Hayrapetyan), 144 (Moment Open/Iqbal Khatri), 150/151 (Corbis/Atlantide Phototravel), 152/153 (Moment/Waitforlight), 154/155 (Universal Images Group/Godong), 158 (Moment/Tran Vu Quang Duy), 159 (Universal Images Group/Godong), 165 top (Moment/Vincent Jary), 167 (Moment Unreleased/Ryan Ang), 170 (E+/Xavierarnau), 171 bottom (Moment Unreleased/Ivan), 186 (Universal Images Group/Eye Ubiquitous), 206 top (Moment Open/Brendan Van Son), 207 top (Moment/Irene Becker Photography), 216/217 (500PxPlus/Dereje Belachew)

iStock: 38 (Letty17)

Shutterstock: 7 (Sursad), 8 (Valerio Mei), 12 (Andy J Billington), 15 bottom (R Martin Seddon), 16 (Attila Jandi), 18/19 (Madrugada Verde), 21 both (Christophe Cappelli), 22 (Grzegorz Pakula), 24 top (Jorn Pilon), 24 bottom (Andre Quinou), 25 (Samot), 26/27 (Tupungato), 30/31 (Vlad G), 32 (Jose Ignacio Soto), 33 (CLS Digital Arts), 34/35 (Pavel Ilyukhin), 36 (Ross Helen), 37 top (Vladimir Sazonov), 37 bottom (Grafalex), 42 (Cge2010), 43 (Karalenkava), 44/45 (Kumpel), 46 (Roberto La Rosa), 49 (Grisha Bruev), 51 bottom (Gnoparus), 53 (VIS Fine Art), 56 (Toporkova), 57 (Kostin SS), 61 (Kamira), 62/63 (Frimufilms), 66 top (Dan Hanscom), 68/69 (Luis Enrique Torres), 73 (Bandersnatch), 74/75 (Chintla), 84/85 (Action Sports Photography), 87 (Anne Beruldsen), 88/89 (Nagel Photography), 91 top (Harold Stiver), 91 bottom right (EQRoy), 93 (Sean Pavone), 94 (Sharkshock), 95 top (Phil Reid), 98 (Jess Kraft), 99 top (Shipfactory), 99 bottom (Cezary Wotjkowski), 100/101 (Eleni Mavrandoni), 105 top (Aleksandr Rybalko), 108/109 (Rafal Cichawa), 110 (Lingling7788), 111 top (Gianfranco Vivi), 114/115 (ScottYellox), 116 (Victor1153), 118/119 (Anton Ivanov), 123 (Vinicius Bacarin), 131 top (Reisegraf.ch), 132 (Artincamera), 134 (Lu Quyen), 138 (eFesenko), 140 top (MehmetO), 140 bottom (Ivachshin), 141 (Vitaliy Maslov), 142/143 (Ravshan Mirzaitov), 145 (A M Syed), 156 (Maki Shunnosuke), 157 (Topimages), 160/161 (Pasakorn Hansetagan), 162/163 (Pipat Kamma), 166 (Randy Pr), 168 top (Sergey-73), 169 (Randy Imanuel), 171 top (Claudine Van Massenhove),172/173 (Boyloso), 174/175 (Marco Ramerini), 178 top (Cezary Wojtkowski), 185 top (Photo Oz), 185 bottom(Valery Voennyy), 190/191 (Khaled El Adawy), 195 (Lisa S), 203 (Homo Cosmicos), 204/205 (Fabian Plock), 207 bottom (Andre Silva Pinto), 212/213 (Cezary Wojtkowski), 222 (Michail Vorobyev), 223 (Trevor Kittelty)